John A. "Snowshoe" Thompson

Pioneer Mail Carrier Of The Sierra

Frank Tortorich

Copyright 2015 Frank Tortorich

ISBN #978-1-941052-09-9-Trade Paper

Library of Congress Control Number: 2015948484

All rights reserved.
No part of this book may be reproduced or transmitted in any
form or by any means, electronic or mechanical,
including photocopying, recording or by any
information storage and retrieval system
without written permission
from the publisher.

Cover Design: Antelope Design
Cover Photo: Frank Tortorich

www.pronghornpress.org

Portrait of John A. "Snowshoe" Thompson
Courtesy: Western American SkiSport Museum

Dedicated to
Nina Eggen MacLeod,
the inspiration for the book

Nina Eggen MacLeod in Norway
Courtesy: Nina Eggen MacLeod

Translation of Monuments

Plaque on the left stone:
SNOWSHOE THOMPSON
THE SKI HERO
From Sierra Nevada
Genoa, USA

Right stone:
Here in
LURÅS-RUE
he was born
JON TORSTEINSON RUE
1827-1876

*History is a jig-saw puzzle.
Today, new pieces give us
a greater understanding
of the life of pioneers
like Snowshoe.*

This quote, by an unknown author, was taken from the program narrative for the Snowshoe Thompson plaque dedication, September 18, 2004, in Genoa, Nevada, celebrated by both the Evangelical Lutheran Church in America and the Lutheran Churches of Scandinavia.

Table of Contents

List of Illustrations xiii

Preface xvii

Acknowledgments xxi

Editorial Considerations xxvii

Introduction xxix

1
Norway 1

2
Early Life in America 11

3
Gold Fever Draws John to California 15

4
A brief History of the United States Mail on the California Trail 34

5
John Thompson Delivers the Mail 49

6
"Snowshoe," the Man 72

7
John Thompson Other Endeavors 100

8
John "Snowshoe" Thompson and the Birth of Ski Racing. 124

9
Snowshoe Thompson Was Never Paid…or Was He? 140

10
Thompson's Last Years 177

11
John Snowshoe Thompson Remembered 196

Appendices 255

Endnotes 267

BIBLIOGRAPHY   279

INDEX   287

ILLUSTRATIONS

Portrait of John A. "Snowshoe" Thompson
frontispiece

Nina Eggen MacLeod in Norway
dedication page

A Stave Church in Norway
2

Laurås Family Crest
6

Map of Journey From Norway
7

Map of Travels in America
10

Thompson Skiing Downhill With a Pole
26

Original Snowshoe Thompson Skis
El Dorado Historical Museum
27

Snowshoe Thompson Skis
Genoa Museum
30

Original Placerville Post Office Site
50

Thompson's Winter Mail Delivery Route
56

Cottage Rock, c 1910
79

Snowshoe Thompson Cave
80

Thompson's Certificate of Citizenship
107

Thompson's Cabin
109

Thompson-made Rocking Chair
109

Portrait of Arthur Thompson
114

Arthur's Cradle Made by Thompson
115

Chorpenning's Mail Delivery Routes
138-139

Headstone of John A. "Thomson"
189

Headstone of "Arthure"
(misspelled on headstone)
191

John Scossa and Agnes Scossa
193

Headstone of Agnes Singleton Thompson Scossa
194

The Thompson Family Plot
195

E. Clampus Vitus (ECV) Marker
in Diamond Valley
199

Native Sons of Golden West (NSGW)
Marker in Diamond Valley
200

Diamond Valley with
ECV and NSGW Markers
200

Statue of Snowshoe Thompson
at Boreal Ski Resort
213

ECV Snowshoe Thompson Monument
at Carson Pass
219

ECV Carson Pass Monument
Dedication Program Cover
222

ECV Snowshoe Thompson Plaque
at Genoa Museum
229

Statue of Snowshoe Thompson
at Mormon Station
237

Plaque at Statue of Snowshoe Thompson
238

Plaque in Front of Headstone
at Thompson's Grave
243

Rue Farm, Norway
245

Author with Statue of Snowshoe Thompson
at Squaw Valley Ski Resort
249

Snowshoe Thompson Ski-Snowshoe Tour
in Hope Valley
251

Preface

As a fourth generation Californian and native of Jackson in Amador County, I was steeped in the history of Kit Carson, emigrant wagon trains over Carson Pass, and the Gold Rush. It was difficult to hike, fish, or hunt in the area without being aware of the rich history that abounded.

In 1978, while still working as an educator in rural Amador County, I became increasingly fascinated with the history of Carson Pass, which is now traversed by modern day CA SR 88. Glenn Gottschall, Amador District Ranger of the Eldorado National Forest, United States Forest Service (USFS), asked my wife, Mary Ann, and me to become official volunteers with the forest service. This enabled us to do research on the Carson River Route of the California Emigrant Trail, and fill a need for the forest service by documenting its history. It seems that the forest service had very little knowledge of the trail and they did not fully understand its historical importance.

Mary Ann and I were delighted to be asked. We started with field research, such as physically locating the trail on the ground, which led us to exciting, but tedious, document research in libraries, museums, and archives. This research eventually led me to write two emigrant trail historical guidebooks, which covered the Carson Pass area where today CA SR 88 crosses the Sierra Nevada. Being a westward migration student and researcher for over thirty-five years, there still remained many puzzle pieces missing in my knowledge of the history of the West.

One of those pieces was the life story of John A. "Snowshoe" Thompson, that incredible mailman of the Sierra. How could this Norwegian deliver the mail from Placerville, California, to Genoa, Nevada, in the dead of winter over the deep snows of Sierra in a five-or-six-day round trip when others could not make it one way without struggling for weeks?

So, for the last ten years, when people asked me what subject I was researching for my next book, I told them "Snowshoe Thompson." Their usual response was, "Oh, I've heard about him." However, when I asked them what they knew about Thompson, they would come back with, "Not very much." Of course, there are those others who would say, "Who?" This spurred me to work on this in-depth study of the man.

Obviously, I wanted—and needed—to know more about this Snowshoe Thompson and his place in history. What was his connection with Post Office Department?

In my research I found a few books written about Snowshoe Thompson, some of which were written for children. It is understandable that those authors would not be concerned about documentation or see a need to provide details or cite sources.

The few other books I found about him did not have the information I felt was necessary to tell the more complete and accurate account of the unique and amazing John A. "Snowshoe" Thompson. Much of what had been written about him was oral history—laced with myth—covering the various aspects of Thompson's life in the United States and his birth home in Norway. However, most did include his heroics as a mailman for twenty years.

Thompson's birthplace was in Norway, so naturally, some of the documents and writings are in Norwegian. These Norwegian studies are mostly limited to Thompson's homeland connection, with just a bit about his American adventures.

The Norwegians hold John Thompson in high esteem, regarding him as a hero. Not only have they written about him, they have also erected many monuments in his honor, and hold annual celebrations. I believe these honors are well deserved.

Acknowledgments

Nina Eggen MacLeod, of South Lake Tahoe, California, is a native of Norway. I cannot thank her enough for her encouragement. The help she provided in locating Norwegian documents and translating them for me has been invaluable. Her assistance with the historic background of the times in Norway during Jon Anon Torsteinsson's formative years was extremely useful. Other than my own curiosity, she was the strongest driving force behind the writing of this book.

Nina has organized and conducted the annual Snowshoe Thompson Tour in Hope Valley, California, every March since 1999. She has never failed to invite me to speak on Snowshoe Thompson for this ski/snowshoeing event. Of course, the more times I spoke, the more I realized I had more questions, which led me to more and more libraries, museums, and archives, seeking answers. Wherever I went, I was met with encouragement and people who were anxious to assist me in my research.

Jeffery M. Kintop, manager at the Nevada

State Library and Archives in Carson City, graciously opened his files to me. Nancy Thornburg, volunteer manager at the Alpine County Archives in Markleeville, California, was most helpful in locating Thompson's land records and more than willing to direct me to other sources. Dick Edwards, of the Alpine County Museum in Markleeville, not only opened the files, but helped with photocopying many pages of documents and records, including a copy of Thompson's Certificate of Citizenship.

For the staff at the National Archives in Washington, D.C., I remain grateful for their expertise in locating and mailing several hundred pages of mail contracts and court cases involving George Chorpenning, the man who held the U.S. mail delivery contracts. He was the man who, according to my research, should have been the one to pay Thompson. I add my continued thanks to the staff of the California Room in the California State Library in Sacramento for all their assistance.

Shannon Van Zant, with the Calaveras County Archives, was gracious and very helpful in allowing me to examine, page by page, years of the *San Andreas Independent* issues and in directing me to other documents in her office. Amanda Mason and Moira Conlan, of the Yolo County Library and Archives, were of tremendous assistance. Thank you.

It is difficult to give a sufficient amount of praise to Ellen Osborn and Mary Cory, of the El Dorado County Historical Museum, for their help and friendship. My friend and Clamper member, Ford Osborn, provided information and background about the extraordinary behavior of E Clampus Vitus. I gratefully acknowledge his help.

Thank you to Eloise James of Pioneer, California, who graciously donated her Snowshoe Thompson collection for my research. To Billie Jean Rightmire, historian for the Genoa Courthouse Museum, Genoa, Nevada, for guiding me to her research documents and granting permission for their use. Ellen Martin, curator at the Carson Valley Museum and Cultural Center in Gardnerville, Nevada, was most gracious in helping me by opening their research files to me and granting me permission for their use in this publication. She also helped me earlier, in her capacity as curator at the Alpine County Museum in Markleeville, California.

Bill Clark of the Western American SkiSport Museum at Boreal Ski Resort, Soda Springs, California, brought out their collection of historic photographs and documents of Snowshoe Thompson, which showed his impact on the ski sport industry. I offer my gratitude.

I am indebted to my Oregon-California Trails Association (OCTA) friends who have provided much appreciated assistance: Dave Bigler for help with the connection Thompson's mother and sister had with the Church of Jesus Christ of the Latter Day Saints (LDS, also referred to as the Mormons); George Ivory for research at the LDS Family Library in Salt Lake City, Utah; our OCTA friend, Richard Wilkes of East Sussex, England, for his research tracing Agnes Singleton's roots in the United Kingdom; and all the other members whose brains I have picked over the years.

I want to thank another dear friend, Keith Davis, for accompanying me to the California State Library to assist in my research and for advising me on the Indian encounters Thompson experienced. To Donnie LeDesma, my Mission Indian friend, for his expertise and help in my endeavors to present the Paiute War of 1860 with a fair and balanced perspective. My appreciation to Wanda Coyan for her assistance with the newspaper files in the Alpine County Museum. To Mary Heidecker of the Amador County Archives for introducing me to *Ghost of the Sierra Nevada: Silver Mountain City*, written by Karen Dustman. Thanks to Karen and her husband, Rick, for their generous support.

Special thanks go to Sue Knight and Nina Eggen MacLeod for proofreading my manuscript and offering their sage advice. They also helped fill in information with "Friends of Snowshoe Thompson" activities and history and supplied photos of events for the book.

I cannot forget my friend, Bob Clark of Arthur H. Clark Company, an imprint of the University of Oklahoma Press, who has shown great confidence in my abilities. He has encouraged me, and politely—sometimes most persistently—prodded me until I finished this study on Snowshoe Thompson and the U.S. mail.

My gratitude to fellow researchers of Snowshoe Thompson, Sharlene Nelson and the late Ted Nelson, from Federal Way, Washington, for their generous sharing of information.

Two other ladies without whom you would not be reading this book are Jo Johnston, my editor who picked me up when I was discouraged, and offered to use this book as a guinea pig to learn a new software program, InDesign, and her friend and publisher of Pronghorn Press, Annette Chaudet. You both were, and remain, special in my heart for believing in the value of this book. Thank you.

Finally, I want to acknowledge my loving wife and best friend, Mary Ann. She serves as my initial editor, proofreader, advisor, research assistant, computer whiz, and cheerleader.

If I have failed to mention anyone by name, I apologize, as without the support of all of you, this work could have never happened.

Frank Tortorich

Editorial Considerations

Numerous documents were used in this study. These include newspaper articles, archival papers, letters, commemorative plaques, monuments, and information obtained from court records.

The choice to use footnotes is to enable the reader immediate explanation of unfamiliar locations, terms, possibly confusing or misleading text, or to add complementary text.

The choice to use endnotes is to document the details of the reference sources being listed, without interrupting the flow of the text.

Original spellings and punctuation have been retained. Other explanations of aides used in this book are:

- [*sic*] indicates a word or term where the original spelling was an actual typographical error, or was an improper use of a word or term. An example: the common misuse of the term "Sierra Nevada mountains" is incorrect and redundant as "Sierra" means "mountains." (There is also a common misuse of the term "Sierras," since "Sierra" is a plural noun.)

- [ ] indicates clarification of the spelling of a word, a person, place, or item, or to clarify wording that otherwise might lead to confusion inside quoted material.

- Carson Valley refers to the land from the base of the Woodfords Canyon in California where the west fork of the Carson River drops into the valley, and north to the ridge of mountains before Carson City, Nevada. Carson City is in Eagle Valley.

- U.S. Postal Service, U.S. Mail Department, etc., are various names used by different authors. I use the name "Post Office Department" to refer to this sector of the U.S. government.

- Lake Valley refers to South Lake Tahoe.

- There are many other spellings of Thompson's Norwegian last name. I have chosen to take the lead from the genealogy work completed by Alverna (Thompson) Robinson and Dorothy Foss in their *History of The Rue Family, 1759-1984* and will use the spelling "Torsteinsson."

John A. "Snowshoe" Thompson
Pioneer Mail Carrier of the Sierra

Introduction

I do not consider the job of a mailman to be a very romantic or exciting profession. As a young boy, growing up in the foothills of northern California, I never thought that being a mailman—a person who walked (or now drives) his appointed route—was something I wanted to do for a living. I wanted to do something more exciting, like be a jet pilot, or a motorcycle police officer.

However, nowadays most of us would agree that without the daily mail delivery our lives, as we know them, could not function. Today I have a great appreciation for the mail delivery service to my front door. Every day I wait for my mail to arrive, as I am sure others do. I am also sure that many people do not have the opportunity to learn the name of their mail delivery person. Fortunately, I do know the name of our mail carrier; her name is Kathy.

In the nineteenth century, there was at least one mailman who made mail delivery an exciting, romantic, and incredibly important profession. That man, of course, was John "Snowshoe" Thompson. He did what no other man had been able to accomplish up until that time; he carried the mail over the Sierra in the dead of winter. He traveled from Placerville, California, to Genoa (Utah Territory) a distance of some eighty-plus miles.* Not only did Thompson carry the mail in winter, but he also accomplished the entire round trip in the phenomenal time of five or six days.

Over the years, we have had many types of mail options. There is snail mail, E-mail, priority mail, bulk mail, parcel post, junk mail, airmail, rail mail, UPS, FedEx, and other services of which I may not be aware. Do not begin to confuse me with the differing rates they charge for each service. All these choices were not available to people in the early to mid-1800s.

At that time in the East, the United States Post Office had established mail roads and routes. In the West, overland mail routes had not been established prior to, or shortly after, the gold discovery of January 24, 1848. Before that time, the only mail delivery from east coast to west coast was by ships sailing from Boston around Cape Horn (the most southern tip of Chile, South America) and up along the coast of Mexico to trade with the people of those countries.

Those ships delivered mail to their ports of call in Alta California (the historic region that contained present-day California and other states to the east of the Rockies), to be picked up by the few Americans living in the Mexican California coastal

---

* Genoa was part of the Utah Territory until 1861 when Nevada became a territory, later becoming a state in 1864.

communities. Some trading ships continued up the coast to the Oregon Territory and delivered mail there. By the mid-1800s, overland mail was carried across the country by the U.S. military—at their convenience—on the backs of mules, sometimes known as "Jackass Mail."

As the country developed, freight wagons and stagecoaches carried mail. Of course, for the eighteen months from April 1860 until October 1861, there was the Pony Express, which continues to fascinate the world to this day. All these delivery methods were slow compared to today's standards.

With the completion of the transcontinental telegraph in 1861, communication changed dramatically. Even though messages could then be sent across the country in seconds, the need for regular mail was still vital. A modern day example would be the way E-mail has changed communication in the late twentieth and twenty-first centuries. Yet, there still remains a need for "snail mail."

At the completion of the transcontinental railroad in 1869, what had been painfully slow, cross-country mail delivery changed into something of "lighting speed" for its day. A letter could travel across the entire country in a matter of days, instead of weeks. Where the train did not run, or when the mail was held up for days due to heavy snow on the tracks, bringing the trains to a standstill, other mail delivery services were still necessary. Delivering mail to isolated areas in the middle of winter became a major challenge for the United States Postal Service (then called U.S. Post Office).

This is where John "Snowshoe" Thompson

made a name for himself by successfully carrying the mail over the Sierra in the dead of winter for twenty years. Those who have written about Snowshoe Thompson and his life and adventures have relied mostly on one interview with him and subsequent stories of Thompson by a journalist using the pen name of "Dan De Quille."

This man, William Wright, was a journalist for the Virginia City (Nevada) newspaper, *The Territorial Enterprise*. He planned to do a series with Thompson, but unfortunately, Thompson died just months after that first interview. De Quille went on to write extensively about Thompson. Being a journalist, not a historian, De Quille did not always get the facts right, or would take editorial license. Later writers perpetuated those mistakes, then repeated them in one publication after another.

De Quille was not the only writer to get things wrong. In reading various documents, I found that authors do not all agree on the details of his life, such as the spelling of Thompson's Norwegian name, or even his American name, or the name of his place of birth, all of which pose problems for the reader. Was his birth name spelled John or Jon? The various spellings of his Norwegian surname led to further confusion. Some authors became confused as to the location of Thompson's home in Norway.

De Quille had him born in "Prestijeld," Norway. There is no such town as Prestijeld.* In my casual reading of all these documents, I became confused, too. Therefore, I began a search to find

---

* The misunderstanding of the use of the word *"Prestegjeld"* is clarified in Chapter 1.

out which were the correct versions. The confusion is now resolved, due to the wonderful and detailed genealogical study by Dorothy Foss and Alverna (Thompson) Robinson, in *History Of The Thompson Rue's Family 1759-1984*, along with the fine work of the Norwegian writer, Jon Haukaas. They have provided a clear and accurate spelling of Thompson's birth name and location of his birth.

There are a limited number of primary sources dealing with Thompson's life in America. Most writers depend on De Quille and newspaper accounts. I have used those, as well, but I have also searched for verification or corrections from other primary sources.

One primary source that holds great credibility for its historical content is the *Knott Reminiscences: Early History of Nevada in the 1850s* by Thomas Knott and edited by Herbert Hamlin.

Hamlin has done a distinct service for Western history in collecting and publishing the records of the pioneers. Much original material has already appeared in Hamlin's periodical, *Pony Express Courier*. These reminiscences of the Nevada pioneer Thomas Knott are especially important and unusual, detailing little known incidents of life at the rugged outpost of Genoa on the eastern slope of the Sierra.

Thomas Knott, like James Marshall, was a millwright who knew how to make a sawmill, a gristmill, or a wagon wheel, using only the most primitive tools and materials. He built many mills, not the least of which was the one at Mormon Station (Genoa). There he lost his son in a Mormon fight, but he held out against great odds when his mill products became vitally necessary to the support of the emigrants at the Washoe Mines.

Dr. Charles L. Camp, a paleontologist at the University of California and a Western historian, edited many pioneer journals and diaries. He wrote the foreword to Knott's reminiscence:

> *His own story, and the recollections of his family, are here gathered together to illuminate a peculiar phase of the Western struggle for existence, when, in the fifties [1850s], Mormons and gentiles clashed on the eastern borders of California.*

This document, overlooked by nearly all other Thompson researchers, was hiding in plain view on a shelf among many other documents in the research room in the Carson Valley Museum and Cultural Center in Gardnerville, Nevada. I also overlooked this important document on my first visit. It was only late into my research that I learned that there might be a connection between Knott and Thompson. I emailed a query to several repositories to see if they had documents making that connection. The only response came from Ellen Martin, the then-curator of the Carson Valley Museum and Cultural Center, saying they had the document I was seeking.

Thomas Knott came to California in 1852 and opened a hardware store in Placerville. It was there he met John Thompson. Knott hired Thompson to work with him to build a sawmill in Carson Valley. Knott told of Thompson delivering mail in the winter over the Sierra on "snowshoes" (skis) several years before being hired by the Post Office Department in 1856.

It is important to note that Thompson was using homemade wooden skis similar to our Telemark skis of today. Early writers used various terms, including "snowshoes," "snow-shoes," or "snow skates." "Snow skates" was the English translation of the Norwegian term for "skis." The reader will see multiple terms used throughout. When referring to Thompson, they always describe his skis.

There are three main goals in this study.

1. To search out as many primary sources as possible.

2. To bring together the numerous stories written over the years about Snowshoe Thompson, and to compare the various inconsistencies in an attempt to find the correct historical information.

3. To answer the question, "Why was he never paid for his twenty years of dedicated mail delivery service in the dead of winter?"

Other questions investigated.

- Who was this extraordinary man named "Snowshoe Thompson?"

- Where did he come from?

- How did he become a mailman?

- Why is there so much confusion by writers as to Thompson's Norwegian name?

- How did he gain the nickname "Snowshoe" Thompson?

- How did the postal route in the West come to be?

- Who ran these dangerous mail routes from the western border of the United States at the Missouri River to California?

John A. "Snowshoe" Thompson

Pioneer Mail Carrier Of The Sierra

JOHN A. "SNOWSHOE" THOMPSON
PIONEER MAIL CARRIER OF THE SIERRA

1

NORWAY

John A. Thompson* was born on the Rue farm in Tinn, Telemark, Norway, on April 30, 1827.[1] All the sources seem to agree on this birth date, but there is some confusion among writers as to the name of his birthplace.

William Wright, a journalist for the *Territorial Enterprise* in Virginia City, Nevada, writing under the pen name "Dan De Quille," interviewed Thompson just months before Thompson's death on May 15, 1876. He published several stories about John "Snowshoe" Thompson based on that single interview and other sources. Many biographers have used De Quille's writings as a primary source for their work. The vast majority of De Quille's work is accurate and reliable, only as long as it can be corroborated by other

---

* John eventually took this name in America. Why the family took the Thompson name is not known, but it may be that it was similar to their Norwegian name.

NORWAY

sources. However, De Quille was a journalist writing his articles to sell. In that capacity he may have used some creativity in his writings to make the stories more appealing to publishers and readers alike.

An example would be De Quille's error in his statement on Thompson's birthplace, which he claimed was at upper Tinn in Prestijeld, Norway.[2] The correct spelling is *"prestegjeld,"* which is translated to mean "parish of the Priest,"[3] or church parish—not a town. It is a geographic and administrative

A Stave Church in Norway
Courtesy Douglas County Historical Society

John A. "Snowshoe" Thompson
Pioneer Mail Carrier of the Sierra

area of the Church of Norway, roughly equivalent to a parish, which could contain many churches or congregations. Norway is geographically divided into 1,298 *prestegjeld* or parishes.*[4]

It is not clear how De Quille came upon this error, although it is possible that he did not understand what Thompson was telling him about his childhood in Norway. Maybe De Quille mistakenly confused the parish name for the town of Thompson's birth.

There seems to be disagreement, or perhaps confusion, with some authors on Thompson's exact birth name.

John A. Thompson was born with the Norwegian name of Jon Anon Torsteinsson Rue.[5] Jon (or John's) father's name was Torstein Olsson Gallo (born 1759). It was common practice to name a male child after the father's first name attaching "son." In this case, his last name became Torsteinsson, which is to say, Jon became the "son of Torstein."†[6] His first name, Jon, came from his maternal grandfather.[7]

It was also the custom in Norway to attach the place where one lived to one's last name. Thompson grew up on the Rue farm in Tinn / Austbygd,‡[8] Telemark, Norway. Therefore, it would have been proper to call him Jon Anon Torsteinsson Rue.

---

* "In the old days it was difficult to travel long distances to get to church, and as a result a *prestegjeld* (clerical district) would build more than one church."

† In the Robinson and Foss genealogy, Jon's name was spelled Torsteinsson, for son of Torstein. Therefore, in this book Torsteinsson will be used.

‡ Rue is derived from an old Norse word "rudit," which means "clearing in the woods."

NORWAY

Jon's mother's name was Gro [pronounced Grŭ] Jonsdatter[9] or Gro Einungbrekke[10]. The eldest child of Jon Ingebritson Einungbrekke and Gyri Sigurdasdatter Bjornerud, she was born in 1781. Just as John Thompson's name appears in several forms, so does Gro's. "Jonsdatter" means "daughter of Jon."* In the genealogical record, she was listed as Gro Jonsdatter Einungbrekke.[11]

In the complexity of all this Norwegian naming, the important piece of the puzzle was that Gro married Torstein in 1812. This was the second marriage for Torstein and the first for Gro. Torstein was first married to Kjersti Rue in 1794. She inherited the Rue farm from her father, Tore. Kjersti died in 1809, devastating Torstein, who was then fifty years old, leaving him to raise their seven children.[12] The economic times were so bad he had to sell the farm and became a tenant farmer.[13]

It is not clear exactly when and why Gro came to live on the Rue farm,[14] † but the speculation is that she was hired by Torstein to be his housekeeper and to care for the children.[15]

On April 16, 1812, Gro married Torstein and they had five additional children: Kjersti (named after Torstein's first wife), was born September 16, 1812;‡ Birgit, was born August 5, 1814; Jon, was born

---
* MacLeod, translation.
† Gro was the second cousin to Kjersti
‡ Author's observation: Gro and Torstein were married April 16, 1812, and Kjersti was born September 16, 1812.

4

John A. "Snowshoe" Thompson
Pioneer Mail Carrier of the Sierra

November 11, 1817 (died at an early age); Torstein, was born October 19, 1819; Kari, was born June 1822; and Jon, was born April 30, 1827.*[16]

Note: It was common practice to name the next child of the same gender after a deceased child.

Life on the Rue farm was difficult for Gro and Torstein, as it was for all tenant farmers in Norway. During that period, the entire country was suffering from continual economic depression.[17] Norway was primarily an agricultural country. It was an independent, but economically poor society, except for the landowners. Norway manufactured few, if any, goods to be traded with other countries and had to import items that could not be obtained by their own resources. Severe winter conditions and wet summers, along with its far north latitude, made farming difficult for most people.

Families raised their own food and were able to eke out a meager living. Sheep, cows, goats, and horses, along with farming and lumbering, were the main means of livelihood. Most Norwegian men developed carpentry and blacksmithing skills, while the women were homemakers developing competence in cooking, weaving, and tailoring.

Between 1815 and 1865, the population of Norway doubled from 900,000 to 1.7 million.† This increase in population further exacerbated an already depressed situation. The increasing population

---

* This last child named Jon became known as John "Snowshoe" Thompson.

† Nina MacLeod, a native-born Norwegian, provided the statistics and the historical perspective in Norway during the early to mid-1800s.

Norway

of tenant farmers, or "cotter-class," suffered the most, which made life for those people in Norway exceedingly difficult, if not unbearable.

Gro, Torstein, and their children endured the same economic difficulties plaguing the rest of the country. During the long winter months, handcrafted snow skates* were the only means of transportation. Children were given snow skates as soon as they could walk, developing the skills of balance, maneuvering, and sliding down hills early in their childhood.[18] Torstein and his older sons would leave home on snow skates and travel west over the mountains to trade for and buy needed goods from ships from other countries at the fjord ports. This trip, or *nordmannsslepa*,† [19] which could take days, was taken winter and summer.[20]

The hard life in Norway was the cause of death

Laurås Family Crest
Source unknown

---

* Skis in the 1850s in California were referred to as "snowshoes." The English translation from Norwegian was "snow skates." They should not be confused with the Canadian-style webbed snowshoes. Today we know them as skis.
† Refers to dragging or pulling.

John A. "Snowshoe" Thompson
Pioneer Mail Carrier of the Sierra

of many, including children. Those who survived were hardy, robust people, adapted to the harsh conditions of their environment. In 1829 Torstein's oldest son, Hølje (by Torstein's first wife Kjersti), died at the age of twenty-one.[21] This son's death and the state of the economy appeared to be too great for Torstein to bear, because not long after Hølje died, Torstein also died at the age of seventy.[22]

Jon, the youngest of Torstein and Gro's five children, was only two years old.[23] Without

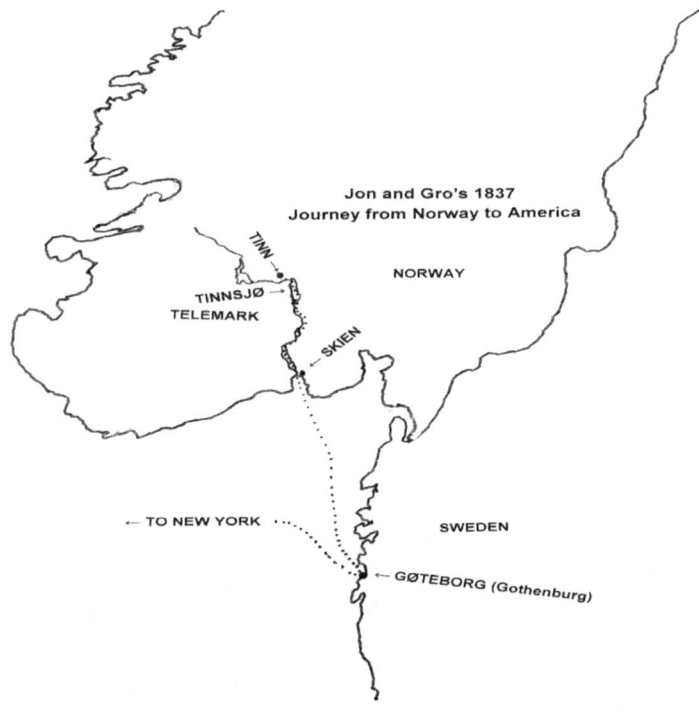

Map of the journey from Norway   *Courtesy: Author*

Torstein, Gro could not stay at the Rue farm and meet the expenses. She was forced to move to a tiny *husmannsplass*, meaning a "hired man's place," that belonged to the Rue family, down by the Lurås River.[24] The name of this place was Vårkåse, meaning "spring in the grove."* [25]

By 1837, life in Tinn had not improved, and Gro, along with her son Jon and others from the area, planned to leave for America. The group began their journey by boat, heading southward on Tinnsjø on May 17, 1837, to Skein. From Skein, on May 22 they sailed for Gothenburg (Gøteborg), Sweden, where they secured passage aboard the Swedish brig, *Njord*.[26] This note appeared in a weekly for *Skein and Environs* on May 23, 1837: "Yesterday fifty-six people from Tinn set sail from here in order to find a brighter future in North America."

The group reached New York on August 15, 1837. In Chicago in early September, the group received assistance from other Norwegians, who had arrived a few years earlier. Their journey continued on to the Fox River settlement in La Salle County, Illinois, where they found new homes.[27]

This "Rue" party, comprised of Gro and her ten year old son Jon, were part of the first group of Norwegians to come to America from eastern Norway. However, they were not the first Norwegians to arrive in that area. Three years earlier in 1834[28] Norwegians from the western part of Norway had settled the Fox River settlement in Illinois.

In 1839, only two years after Gro and Jon first

---

* Even though there are no buildings left, the location is still known by the family.

John A. "Snowshoe" Thompson
Pioneer Mail Carrier of the Sierra

arrived in New York, two of her other children arrived in America: twenty year old Torstein Torsteinsson and seventeen year old Kari. Gro's two other children, Kjersti and Birgit, married and remained in Norway.[29]

Early Life in America

Map of Travels in America *Courtesy: Author*

John A. "Snowshoe" Thompson
Pioneer Mail Carrier of the Sierra

2

Early Life in America

Not much is known about the life of Jon Torsteinsson and his family after their arrival in Illinois. Several researchers have given similar, but varying, accounts of their moving about during their early years in America.

Dan De Quille wrote:* "The family made Illinois their first halting place, but in 1838 they left that state and went to Missouri. In 1841, the family left Missouri and went to Iowa, where they remained until 1845, when they returned to Illinois."

By 1846, Gro, at age sixty-five, had lived

---

*Dan De Quille interviewed John "Snowshoe" Thompson in 1876 while writing for the *Territorial Enterprise* newspaper (Virginia City, Nevada), published during the Comstock Lode mining era beginning in 1859. Mark Twain (Samuel Langhorne Clemens) was a friend of Dan De Quille (William Wright) who also wrote for the *Territorial Enterprise*.

Early Life in America

through many hardships. There are conflicting stories concerning what happened to Gro. "The centennial history of the township of Springdale, Illinois, states that Gro joined the Mormon converts going to Salt Lake City where she lived until her death."*[1]

Dr. Kenneth O. Bjork provided this account, quoting Hjalmar Rued Holand:†[2] "The family went to the Fox River settlement in Illinois, and in 1838 formed a part of a group that founded the first Norwegian settlement in Shelby County, Missouri... The Rues left Missouri in 1840 and settled at Sugar Creek, Iowa, where their mother died."

Jon Haukaas wrote: "The settlers were dissatisfied with the wilderness... Missouri has never been a state for the Norwegian. It was a slave state, and the people of Norway hated Slavery."

Robinson and Foss noted: "Several sources state that Gro became a Mormon, either at Fox River or at Sugar Creek. Ole Olsson, the Lutheran lay preacher whom Jon lived with at Fox River, became a leader among the Norwegian Mormons for a time. It may be because of his influence that Gro joined the group."

Yet another account written of Gro's life by Gene Estensen‡ [3] presents a bit of a different story:

---

*Several sources say she died at Sugar Creek, Iowa, while others state she joined the Mormon Church and went West.
† Hjalmar Rued Holand was an early advocate of Vikings who had appeared in the new world five hundred years before Columbus. Holand immigrated to America in 1884 and received a BA and MA from the University of Wisconsin in 1898.
‡Gene Estensen, a descendant from Tinn families has researched and written articles for the *Telesoga*, a journal for the Norwegian Heritage organization, Teleaget of America, Hudson, Wisconsin.

John A. "Snowshoe" Thompson
Pioneer Mail Carrier of the Sierra

"In 1846 she [Gro] became part of the Blue Mounds settlement in Dane County, Wisconsin. Her son Torstein [Jon's older brother who came to America in 1839] settled at Blue Mounds and the author [Estensen] believes that the widow Rue [Gro] was with him."

Estensen also believed that Jon remained with them until 1851 when he departed for California.

Jon Haukaas asked the question of what became of Jon's sister: "Did she (Kari) marry a young Norwegian Mormon and go west? We do not know." We could speculate that if Gro became a Mormon and went to the Great Salt Lake, it would be logical that Kari followed her mother's example by becoming a Mormon and moving west to be with her mother.

In either 1841 or 1843, Tore Røysland, Jon and Torstein's half-brother, immigrated to America and settled in Wisconsin.

It might have been during this time that the family Americanized the name to Thompson. Jon would now take on the name John A. Thompson.* It is not certain what this letter "A" represents. Some say Anon,† [4] others Alfred, or Arthur. Evelyn Dangberg Teal, in the footnotes in her book about Thompson, wrote that his middle name was "Albret," saying that is how it appeared in the family Bible, which was written by John himself.[5]

Later in California, John married and had a son he named Arthur. So, possibly, in keeping with

---

* In this book, from this page forth, Jon Torsteinsson Rue will be referred to as John Thompson, unless Jon is used in a direct quote.

†Anon is listed as John's middle name, Jon Anon Torsteinsson Rue in Chapter 14 of the Teal study.

Early Life in America

his Norwegian tradition, he named his son after himself, and in following American tradition, used his own middle name for his son. Or, perhaps John did not signify anything at all with the letter A.⁶

Jon Haukaas has given us some insight as to what John did with his time and how he made a living during the mid to late 1840s.

> *We have very little knowledge of Jon's living the years he stayed in Wisconsin. He did not purchase land, as far as we know he was a day laborer. He—like other day-laborers—found employment at farmer's hay making and harvesting. During the winter, he worked in the woods, with cutting, chopping, teaming or other works. And they went into well-digging. John was a handy and dexterous man and we presume that he did carpentry. It is also told that he went out hunting.*⁷

With his mother either dead, or having moved west with the Mormons, Thompson must have been getting restless. With no reason to stay in Wisconsin, it seems that Thompson heard the call of the California gold fields.

JOHN A. "SNOWSHOE" THOMPSON
PIONEER MAIL CARRIER OF THE SIERRA

3

GOLD FEVER DRAWS JOHN THOMPSON TO CALIFORNIA

With the discovery of gold in California,[*] the end of the War with Mexico,[†] the idea of "Manifest Destiny,"[‡] and the realization of California's potential, talk of gaining the great wealth in this military possession of California must have been part of everyone's conversation.

---

[*] Gold was discovered on January 24, 1848, by James Marshall while he was inspecting the trail race for a sawmill he and John Sutter were building in Coloma, California.

[†] The Treaty of Guadalupe Hidalgo was signed on February 2, 1848, later to be ratified by both the U.S. and Mexican Congresses.

[‡] In the 1840s it came to mean that the Americans are destined, by divine providence, to own the country from ocean to ocean. "Manifest Destiny" was a phrase coined by a New York journalist, John O'Sullivan in July 1845.

Gold Fever Draws John Thompson to California

On December 5, 1848, in President James Knox Polk's State of the Union address to congress, he announced a great gold discovery in California. This news soon hit all the Midwestern and Eastern newspapers.

The country was all in a stir.[1] By the spring of 1849, the Gold Rush was on. With so much excitement, men left their farms, families, and businesses, and headed for California to strike it rich. Along with so many other young single men, it would seem only logical that Thompson would be caught up in "Gold Fever." Traveling to California was no longer going to another country, as it had been up until two years earlier, because all land west of the Rocky Mountains now belonged to the United States.

First, on April 30, 1803, there was the Louisiana Purchase—a huge piece of land that encompassed everything west of the Mississippi to the Rocky Mountains.[2] Then on June 18, 1846,[3] the Oregon Territory became part of the United States when Great Britain signed over the Northwest Territory. The last puzzle piece to complete the United States was Alta California, consisting of all the land south of the Oregon Territory, north of the Gila River, and from the Pacific Ocean east to the Rocky Mountains.* On February 2, 1848, with the signing of the Treaty of Guadalupe Hidalgo,[4] the United States of America now owned the land from the Atlantic Ocean to the Pacific Ocean.

California was admitted to the union on

---

* The Gadsden Treaty with Mexico of 1853 finalized the boundary south to the present location between United States and Mexico.

John A. "Snowshoe" Thompson
Pioneer Mail Carrier of the Sierra

September 9, 1850. On that same date, Utah Territory was established. Due to the great wealth from the gold discovery, the U.S. Congress rushed California into statehood without it first being a territory.

Due to the great silver discovery in 1859, the Nevada Territory, carved out of the western part of the Utah Territory, was established on March 2, 1861. On October 31, 1864, Nevada became a state.

That did not mean that the cross-country journey to California would be any easier than it had been in prior years. The main difference was that travelers no longer needed a passport to enter California, nor did they need permission, or a visa, from the Mexican government to stay. The journey still took months of planning and preparation for the travelers' five-month overland trip.

Food, clothing, tools, animals, and wagons all had to be purchased, either new or in top condition. There would be little opportunity for the '49er to resupply along the way, as the few forts or trading posts that did exist could not supply all the travelers' needs. Consequently, gold seekers had to plan to take everything they might need with them.

Little is known about what plans Thompson made in preparation for his trip to California. One source states that Thompson drove a herd of milk cows to California.[5] Another version is that Thompson's half-brother, Tore Røysland had the idea of taking milk cows to California to sell the milk to the miners for an exorbitant price. He asked John to go with him.[6]

In 1849, the number of gold seekers going to California has been estimated to be between

Gold Fever Draws John Thompson to California

25,000 and 40,000 people. 1850 was one of the peak migration years, with numbers estimated between 55,000 and 75,000 people going west to California.[7] However, 1851 would see a drop in the numbers of gold seekers traveling to California, as the number of travelers dropped dramatically to under ten thousand. This could have been because of the large number of fatalities on the trail due to a cholera epidemic in 1850.[8]

The brothers' plan was to travel in the spring of 1851. There is no documentation available to show how John and Tore dealt with the cholera fatality information of the year before, or even if they had that knowledge. Nonetheless, they did strike out for California. Here again, there is no documentation indicating which route they followed.

Did their travels take them to the Salt Lake Valley? With so many Mormons in Illinois, there was a possibility that Thompson's mother and sister might have converted to the Mormon religion. If the women were there, it seems logical that they would have stopped in Salt Lake City to visit them. Regardless, Salt Lake Valley would be a good place to stop to sell some cows* and purchase supplies.

Other questions come to mind. Did they travel by wagon train? If they did not, then they probably would have traveled using pack animals. Also, which route did they travel?

In 1851, there were only two trans-Sierra wagon routes crossings into California. The Truckee River Route, opened in 1844, crossed over the Sierra

---

* No verification has been found whether Thompson and his half-brother arrived in California with the herd of milk cows.

John A. "Snowshoe" Thompson
Pioneer Mail Carrier of the Sierra

on what is presently referred to as the Donner Trail, which closely followed along present day I-80 over Donner Pass. The Donner route would not have taken the men directly to the gold fields. It would have taken them about forty miles north of Sacramento. From there they would have continued south to Sacramento, then east thirty miles to the gold fields in the Coloma and Placerville areas.

The Carson River Route, opened in 1848,[9] crossed over Carson Pass, closely following along the present day CA SR 88. Gold seekers would have used that route as the most direct and shorter route to the same gold fields. Another logical reason gold seekers would have likely used the Carson route is that they would have had only three river crossings in the Carson River canyon, whereas travelers would have had twenty-seven or more river crossings in the Truckee River canyon.[10]

De Quille wrote that Thompson mined for gold in Placerville, Coon Hollow, and Kelsey's Diggings.[11] With this information, it is reasonable to assume they traveled the Carson River Route. This route was considered the best and fastest way to the gold fields. Using either route, Thompson would have been introduced to the rugged topography of the beautiful Sierra.

Although answers to these questions may never be found, it is known that Snowshoe Thompson arrived in California and tried his hand at gold mining. It would appear that he did not do well because, in 1853, he went to work for Thomas Knott.

Thomas Knott and one of his sons, Elzy, came to California in 1852 by way of the Carson River

Gold Fever Draws John Thompson to California

Route, traveling through Eagle Valley (Carson City) and Carson Valley, stopping at Mormon Station (Genoa, Nevada*). After they arrived in Placerville, Knott and his son were hired to work in a hardware store.† [12] Thomas Knott was a millwright by trade.

When he came through Carson Valley and entered the mouth of the Carson River, he was taken with the abundance of timber and the rushing of the Carson River. Knott determined it (Woodfords and the forests by Genoa) was the perfect place to build a sawmill.[13]

In the spring of 1853, Knott decided to leave Placerville and go back over the mountain. He wanted to build sawmills and gristmills in the Carson Valley area. Knott recalled that trip:

> *The next week or two I crossed the Snow Mts. with two others that had snow shoes on. So I followed their tracks and kept myself from sinking in the snow and got over safe. One of these men on snow shoes‡ was a Norwegian; he carried the mail for us the winter before and crossed the Mountains on his snow shoes. We gave him $2.00 a letter, and he made a trip every two weeks.*[14]

---

* Genoa (pronounced jen-NO-ah) was part of the Utah Territory until March 2, 1861, when Nevada became a territory, before becoming the thirty-sixth state on October 31, 1864.

† Thomas Knott left a journal dated January 28, 1881. From June 1934 to May 1944, Herbert Hamlin was the editor of the *Pony Express Courier* and edited Knott's journal. See Appendix B.

‡ The author's assumption is these two men were not on snow skates and Thompson was.

John A. "Snowshoe" Thompson
Pioneer Mail Carrier of the Sierra

Herbert Hamlin* described this same event:

> *During the winter of 1852 and 1853 he and his son, Elzy, operated a small (hardware) store in Hangtown†, mostly mining tools, etc.," says Albert his 98 year old son now living. However, by nature he was a finished millwright, and not a miners' supply merchant. He had noticed the ideal spot for a saw mill surrounded by timber on his way up the West Carson Canyon, and could not wait to get there. Leaving so early in the year to cross the Sierra, when the snows were "two to ten feet deep" was dangerous for one without experience.*
>
> *It is, therefore, quite probable that Snowshoe Thompson was one of the extra men he took along. Thompson had a claim over the hill from Hangtown in Coon Hollow but found little gold. It was that same year, 1853 that he first worked for Knott—whom he referred to as the Norwegian carrying the mail for him on snow shoes at $2.00 a letter. He also told Albert Knott, his son, the same.*

All accounts included in the *Knott Reminisces*

---
* Herbert Hamlin not only interviewed Albert, but also Elzy, Knott's only daughter, Elyzett Knott Selby. These interviews and texts, Thomas's and Albert's reminiscences are included in the *Knott Reminiscences*.

† Hangtown became present-day Placerville. See Appendix C.

Gold Fever Draws John Thompson to California

agreed that Thompson carried the mail for Knott. It is a bit confusing as to the first year did so, as Knott said, "...he carried the mail for us the winter before..."

Speculation from Knott's words could be construed to mean that Knott probably came over in late summer or early fall of 1852. Therefore, in the spring of 1853 he, along with Thompson and a third man, traveled back over the mountain.

Knott stated he carried the mail for "us" the winter before and crossed the mountains on "his snowshoes."* Would that have been the past winter of 1852-1853, from Placerville to Genoa? Or was it the next winter that he carried the mail for Knott in the winter of 1853-54, from Genoa to Placerville? It probably makes more sense, following the sequence of Thompson's travel, that 1853-1854 would be correct winter years.

Either way, this document showed Knott paid Thompson to deliver the mail on snowshoes (snow skates), during the time when snow covered the mountains, and three years before he was hired to deliver the mail for the U.S. Post Office Department between Placerville and Genoa.

After Thompson helped Knott build sawmills, and delivering the mail during that same time period, he went to work on a ranch at Putah Creek in 1854.† One source, Gene Estensen, was of the opinion that Thompson made enough money to purchase the farm and that he lived there for the next few years.[15]

---

* The author assumes "his snow shoes" were "snow skates" known as "skis" in the United States today.
† Putah Creek is in the California Central Valley just west of Sacramento, near the town of Winters.

John A. "Snowshoe" Thompson
Pioneer Mail Carrier of the Sierra

However, after searching Yolo County deed/grant records, no documentation was found showing that anyone named John A. Thompson owned land there.[16] Moreover, his name does not show on any census records in that area during that period.[17]

Without being able to verify the exact ranch location, it would be assumed it was near the town of Winters as that is where, historically, most of the farming activity was found. Confusion remains as to when and how long Thompson lived on the ranch.

According to Dan De Quille, "Thompson lived on his ranch during the years 1854-1855."[18]

From the *Sacramento Union*, dated January 19, 1856, these words appeared, "Mr. John A. Thompson, who resides on Putah Creek, in Yolo County..."

Yet another article, dated April 23, 1857, had Thompson still living on Putah Creek, having the ranch location in Solano County.

> *Mr. Thompson, the Carson Valley Expressman, who has a ranch on the south side of Putah Creek in Solano County, which he left yesterday, informs us that the prospect in the neighborhood is most gloomy. Every species of vegetation is suffering from drought.*[19]

Present day maps of the area show Putah Creek as the boundary between Yolo County to the north and Solano County to the south. Might this have meant that Thompson's ranch could have been on both sides of Putah Creek?

Gold Fever Draws John Thompson to California

In the fall of 1855, while living on Putah Creek, Thompson was reported to have read an article in the *Sacramento Union* requesting a mail carrier to deliver mail from Placerville, California, to Genoa, Utah Territory,* during the winter months when the Sierra was covered with very deep snow. The article from the *Sacramento Union* read:

> People Lost to the World
> Uncle Sam Needs Carrier
>
> *People living east of the Sierra Nevada Mountains [sic] and west of Salt Lake lose contact with the outside world as winter snows cut off all communication. The greatest cry from the people is for mail. Congress passed a bill August 18, 1856 providing for post route from Placerville Calif. to Genoa, Utah Territory. So far, no one has come to accept the mail-carrying job for this year, according to Mr. A.M. Thatcher, postmaster of Placerville.*[20]

Being that Thompson made his first Sierra crossing with the U.S. mail in January of 1856, the date of the bill's passage in congress in this article is problematic. An explanation might be that Thompson was hired to carry the mail in anticipation of congress passing the bill. On the other hand, the newspaper may have just had the wrong date.

---

* In 1855, Genoa was still part of the Utah Territory. Genoa became part of the Nevada Territory when it was formed in 1861. Nevada became a state in 1864.

John A. "Snowshoe" Thompson
Pioneer Mail Carrier of the Sierra

A kink in all of this is that the original quoted article has not yet been located. However, Thompson must have become aware of the need for a winter mail carrier by some means, as he applied for the job and was hired.

As will be explained in Chapter 4, a man named George Chorpenning did hold a mail delivery contract for this route, so he should have been the person to hire Thompson.

In Chapter 9, it will be shown that mail contracts were already in existence, but under a cloud of controversy.

James Mason Hutchings, who came to California in 1849, published De Quille quotes about Thompson remembering his youth in Norway and growing up on snow skates,[21] and that he believed he could travel over the deep Sierra snow.

Thompson started making snow skates (skis)* by hand. The following accounts describe those skis and their use; not all accounts agree on the ski's length or Thompson's design.

In an article in 1857, James Hutchings described the "skates":[22]

> The skate consists of a single piece of strong stiff wood, from six to seven and a half feet in length, that turning up in front six to eight inches terminating in a point, six inches in width on the bottom at the bend gradually tapering backwards to

---
* The Norwegian term for snow skates would be translated to skis today.

Gold Fever Draws John Thompson to California

Thompson Skiing Downhill With a Pole
Courtesy: Western American SkiSport Museum

four inches in width. It is flat on the bottom, the top oval or rounded except about a foot in length where the foot rests, a little back of center, here it is an inch and a half in thickness, from thence tapering to half an inch or less on either end.

The only fastening is a single strap over the toe of the boot admitting the freest possible motion to the feet and ankles. In making progress the skate is only raised from the snow when it is desired to make a shorter turn than would otherwise be possible.

On uphill or level surfaces the skates are placed parallel to each other and pushed forward alternately with ease about the length of an ordinary

John A. "Snowshoe" Thompson
Pioneer Mail Carrier of the Sierra

Author with an Original Pair of Snowshoe Thompson Skis
at El Dorado County Historical Museum

> *step, but the impetus given causes them to slide further than this, while descending surfaces they run with great ease and rapidity, and when the declivity is very great, making it necessary to check the motion by throwing the weight of the skier upon a double handed staff, six feet in length, forcing it into the snow upon one side as showed in the cut.*

Dan De Quille wrote of John Thompson's "snow-shoes":

Gold Fever Draws John Thompson to California

When he was a boy, in Norway, snow-shoes* were objects as familiar to him as ordinary shoes are to children in other lands. He determined to make a pair of snow-shoes out of oak timber he was engaged in splitting. Although he was ten years of age at the time he left his native land, his recollections of the shoes he had seen there were in the main correct.

Nevertheless, the shoes he then made were such as would at the present day be considered much too heavy and somewhat clumsy. They were ten feet in length, were four inches in width behind the part on which the feet rest, and were four inches and a quarter wide... When he reached Placerville, he put them on a pair of scales, and found they weighed twenty-five pounds.[23]

In 1954, Curator Carroll D. Hall,[†24] Sutter's Fort, Sacramento, described Thompson's skis:

A curious pair of skis, said to belong to Thompson may be seen in Sutter's Fort Historical Monument. They have an upsweep in front of 13½ inches. He had other skis.

In the late '60s [1860s], in a

---

* De Quille is calling Thompson's skis "snow-shoes," the term in common usage at that time.

† Carroll D. Hall wrote the preface to the reprint of the 1886 article that Dan De Quille wrote for the *Overland Monthly*.

John A. "Snowshoe" Thompson
Pioneer Mail Carrier of the Sierra

challenge to the "boys" of Plumas and Sierra Counties, Snowshoe Thompson said his "snow-shoes" were 9 feet long, turned in front and flat-bottomed; 4 inches wide in front; 3½ inches behind, and 1 1/2 inches thick in center.[*]

Thompson's skates and his technique on the snow were described by another observer:

Instead of wearing the ordinary snow shoes, the mail carrier uses long wooden skates, common in the north of Europe. These skates are five or six feet in length, turning up in the front like a sleigh runner; the foot is fastened to the board by a leather band, with a ridge under the hallow of the boot, which prevents it from slipping back. Thus prepared with a strong pole to guide him, he slips along over the Archives snow with astonishing speed; on the down grade he rests himself partially on the pole, and slides down the hill as swiftly as a school boy can on his sled.[25]

It is realistic to think that Thompson made several sets of skis over his twenty-year career. With

---

[*] Judy Russo, Registrar for the California State Parks in Sacramento, stated that these skis are no longer in Sacramento, but were transferred in 1961 to Plumas-Eureka State Park in Blairsden, California.

GOLD FEVER DRAWS JOHN THOMPSON TO CALIFORNIA

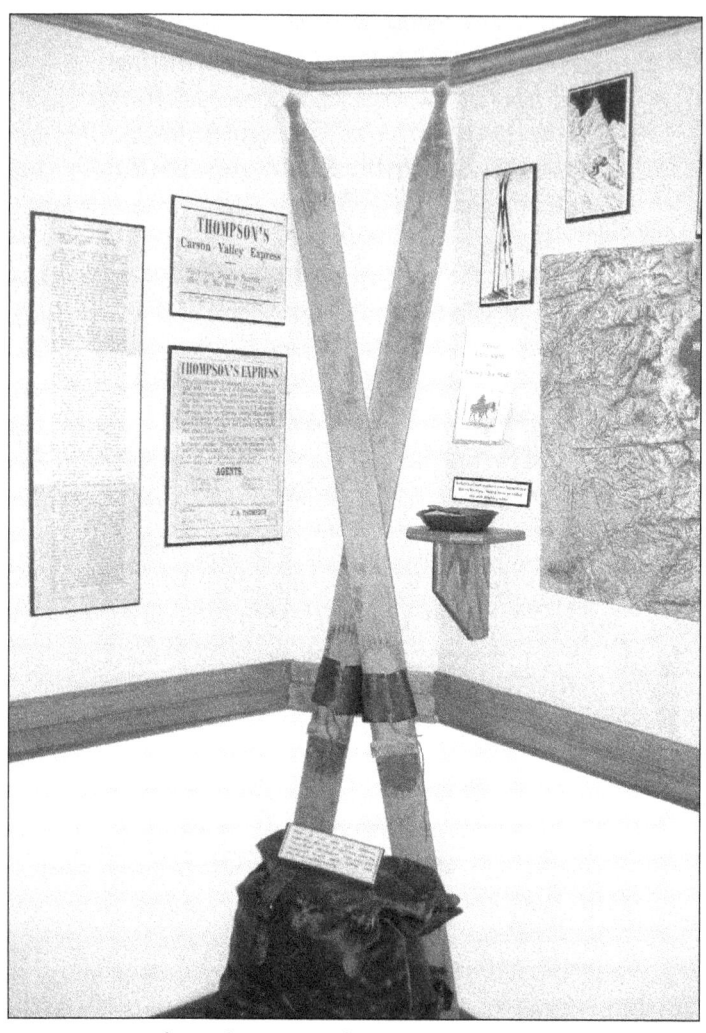

Snowshoe Thompson Skis at Genoa Museum
Photo by Author

John A. "Snowshoe" Thompson
Pioneer Mail Carrier of the Sierra

his skills, it would be logical that he made them many different lengths and designs for various skiing conditions. Perhaps this would account for the wide ranging descriptions of skis that he was purported to wear.

Finishing the construction of this first set of snow skates, Thompson is said to have set out to find some snow to practice on. Just how much practice he needed is pure speculation. He might have made a pair of "snow skates" to use when in Wisconsin and surely used skis while working for Thomas Knott in 1853. Perhaps this "first set of snow skates" was specially designed for the Sierra snow and the steepness and, therefore, he felt the need to test or practice with them.

On the other hand, the heavier and wetter snow in the Sierra Nevada differs greatly from light and very dry snow of the Midwest and the Rocky Mountains. Perhaps, this was the reason Thompson felt he needed practice before applying for the job as mail carrier over the Sierra.

Dan De Quille wrote of Thompson's practice:

Stealing away to retired places near town [Placerville], Thompson spent several days practicing on his snowshoes. His whole soul was in the business, and he soon became so expert that he did not fear letting himself be seen in public on his snowshoes. He was so much at home on

Gold Fever Draws John Thompson to California

them, that he felt he should do no discredit to his native land. When he made his first public appearance, he was already able to perform such feats as astonished all who beheld them. His were the first Norwegian snow-shoes ever seen in California.* [26]

...With his balance-pole in his hand, he dashed down the sides of the mountain at such a fearful rate of speed as to cause the many to characterize the performance as fool-hardy. Not a few of his old friends among the miners begged him to desist, swearing roundly that he would dash his brains out against a tree or plunge over some precipice and break his neck. But Thompson only laughed at their fears. With his feet firmly braced, and his balance-pole in his hands, he flew down the mountain slopes, as much at home as the eagle soaring and circling above neighboring peaks.

Snow-shoe Thompson did not ride astride his guide-pole, nor trail it by his side in the snow, as is the practice of other snow-shoers, when descending a steep mountain, but held it horizontally before him, after the manner of a tight-rope walker. His

---

* From this one statement, it is clear the De Quille was not aware of the Norwegians using snow skates (skis) in the mining community of La Porte, California, in 1853.

JOHN A. "SNOWSHOE" THOMPSON
PIONEER MAIL CARRIER OF THE SIERRA

appearance was most graceful when seen skating down the face of a steep mountain, swaying his long balance pole now to this side and now to that, as a soaring eagle moves its wings.[27]

Therefore, after practicing and gaining confidence in his skiing abilities, Thompson applied for the job at the post office in Placerville with the postmaster.[28]

4

A Brief History of the United States Mail on the California Trail

Why did the Post Office Department never pay Snowshoe Thompson for his twenty years of mail service over the Sierra in winter? To answer that question the necessary foundation is the history of the mail service and mail road contracts.

The Post Office Department predates the 1776 signing of the Declaration of Independence of the United States. In 1691, the last decade of the seventeenth century, King William III granted a twenty-one year postal patent to Thomas Neale to establish postal service among the colonies.[1] In 1753, Ben Franklin was appointed as postmaster general. He improved the service and turned a profit.[2] The

John A. "Snowshoe" Thompson
Pioneer Mail Carrier of the Sierra

postal services for the colonies experienced numerous changes over the next few decades.

In 1772, postal rates for a single letter were as follows:

- Delivered less than thirty miles - $.06
- Delivered thirty miles to sixty miles - $.08
- Delivered between sixty and one hundred miles - $.10
- Delivered between one hundred miles and one hundred and fifty miles - $.12½
- This incremental progression continued until finally, a letter delivered over four hundred fifty miles was $.25[3]

With the development of the American Revolution, the United States Constitution gave congress power to establish post offices and post roads;[4] this Post Office Department was intended to be self-supporting from its very beginning in 1790. There were seventy-five post offices and 1875 miles of post roads; receipts were $37,935 and expenditures were $32,140.

By comparison, sixty years later, in 1850, there were 18,417 post offices and 178,672 miles of post roads; receipts totaled $5,499,984 and expenditures were $5,212,953.[5]

As time went on people became irritated over the high rates for postage.

Brief History of United States Mail on the California Trail

In 1840, England adopted a uniform rate of two cents throughout all of England and Ireland. Due to the success in England, the United States Congress passed a postal rate act on March 3, 1845, establishing the rates for a ½-ounce letter:

- o Delivered under three hundred miles was $.05

- o Delivered over three hundred miles was $.10[6]

Still, not everyone was happy with these new rates and there were more protests. Therefore, on March 3, 1851, congress passed another postal reduction. These new rates for ½-ounce letter were:

- o Delivered less than three thousand miles was $.03

- o Delivered over 3,000 was $.06[7]

The drop in rates would produce a shortfall and congress would have to subsidize the Post Office Department to make up the difference.

Manifest Destiny was fast becoming a reality with the United States about to acquire the Oregon Territory (1846) and soon to be at war with Mexico over California and Texas lands. It was vital to deliver mail to the west side of the continent as quickly and as reliably as possible.

On March 3, 1847, congress passed an act directing the Secretary of the Navy to advertise for

John A. "Snowshoe" Thompson
Pioneer Mail Carrier of the Sierra

bids to carry mail by one steamship between New York and Chagres in central Panama* and by a second ship to carry mail between Panama† and San Francisco, using sailing ships to continue on to Astoria, Oregon Territory.[8] California was still under Mexican rule. It was two years before the steamships would go into service to deliver the mail.‡ [9]

On February 2, 1848, the Unites States took possession of lands won from Mexico with the signing of the Treaty of Guadalupe Hidalgo.[10] That was just nine days after James Marshall discovered gold at Sutter's Mill at Coloma, California, on January 24, 1848. After that, the primary destination for men and ships became not just Oregon, but San Francisco, the gateway to the gold fields. With masses of gold seekers coming to California overland, the need for mail to be delivered to the lonely, homesick men in the gold fields became essential.

Kit Carson and fellow mountain man, Thomas Fitzpatrick, were most likely the first persons to deliver the mail overland to the East. Carson was part of John C. Fremont's third expedition to California in 1845-46. On September 5, 1846, Carson left Los Angeles carrying letters destined for Washington, D.C., describing the Mexican War in California.

---

* The Chagres River meets the Atlantic Ocean at the end of the modern day Panama Canal. See Appendix E.
† Other steamships would pick up the mail in Panama City on the Pacific Ocean. The Panama Canal was completed in 1914.
‡ Bancroft tells the story of the transport of mail and human cargo over the Isthmus of Panama.

Brief History of United States Mail on the California Trail

West of Santa Fe, on his way to deliver these letters, Carson met General Stephen W. Kearny* with the Army of the West, who was heading for California to fight the Mexicans.

Kearny ordered Carson to return to California as his guide. Carson gave the mail to Fitzpatrick to take on east to complete the overland mail delivery.†[11]

On April 17, 1848, Carson was again to deliver mail for the military to Washington, D.C.; this time he made it all the way to Washington.[12] It was highly likely that Carson also carried news of the gold discovery situation in California.

On August 14, 1848, congress passed a postal act directing the Postmaster General to establish post offices in San Diego, Monterey, and San Francisco and to set the postage rates for a half-ounce letter of:

- o $.12½ within California
- o $.40 to the Atlantic Coast.[13]

In 1847, 1848, and part of 1849, the military delivered the mail overland when they traveled from army post to army post across the country. Citizens were able to use this service, along with the soldiers' personal mail.[14] However, there was no scheduled mail delivery, except whenever and wherever the army assignments were ordered. It is not clear just how dependable this army mail delivery was, but, there is some evidence of mail being carried to the East on the California Trail.

In order for the emigrants and '49ers to keep

---

*Kearny is pronounced "Kar-nee"
† Author's note: This could be listed as a two-man Pony Express.

John A. "Snowshoe" Thompson
Pioneer Mail Carrier of the Sierra

in contact with their loved ones back in the States, there were instances of individual people traveling east who provided informal mail service. On June 14, 1849, William Swan wrote his wife, Sabrina from Fort Kearney (Nebraska), that he "was anxious to get the letter in the mail as the mail leaves here every two weeks for Independence [Missouri]."[15]

On July 24, 1847, Brigham Young brought the first group of Mormons into the Salt Lake Valley, to make it their permanent settlement. With family and friends scattered from the Iowa to the valley, it was crucial that mail be delivered all along that trail. The first letters sent east from Salt Lake were carried by Ezra Benson in August of 1847.

There always seems to be someone willing to take advantage of any situation. In 1849, Alonzo Delano wrote in his journal from South Pass (Wyoming), "A sign stood near the road that read 'Post-Office' with a notice that one of the company was leaving for the States and carry letters &c., &c. 'Price, half a dollar.' Many a half dollar was left, but that letter which our company left for their friends never reached them."[16]

In 1849, due to an increasing need for dependable mail delivery, the federal government established a post office in Salt Lake City, appointing J. L. Heywood postmaster.[17]

The Mormons were continuing their migration to Salt Lake Valley, and as previously cited, California was on the brink of statehood. Utah was also close to becoming a U.S. territory. The need for dependable mail service continuing from the East to the West Coast was becoming a dire necessity.

Brief History of United States Mail on the California Trail

In 1850, the Post Office Department provided postal facilities in Utah. Samuel Woodson of Independence, Missouri, was awarded the mail contract to deliver the mail from Salt Lake City east to the Missouri River on a monthly basis.[18] This contract finally succeeded in connecting mail delivery service to the rest of the United States east of the Missouri River.

The only remaining segment not connected by federal mail delivery service was from Salt Lake City to California. Congress pushed for California's statehood with the discovery of gold, and on September 9, 1850, California became the thirty-first state. California is the only state that went from a military possession to statehood without first becoming a territory.

On that very same date, Utah became a territory. It included land east of the present boundary of California to what would eventually become the states of Nevada, Utah, Arizona, and parts of Colorado. After that, it did not take long for the United States to establish a mail route from Salt Lake City to Sacramento.[19]

By that time there were more Americans in California than in Oregon and Utah put together due to the hordes of people with gold fever flooding in to seek their fortune.

Advertisements for the mail contract can be documented as early as January of 1851. Thirty-seven bids were submitted. The winners, with the lowest bid of $14,000 per year, were Absalom Woodward and George Chorpenning. Terms of the contract included the stipulation that mail would be delivered once every thirty days, each way.[20]

Chorpenning and his men left Sacramento on

John A. "Snowshoe" Thompson
Pioneer Mail Carrier of the Sierra

May 1, 1851, with the first mail to Salt Lake City. It took them sixteen days to reach Carson Valley on the east side of the Sierra due to the lingering deep snow. Upon arriving in the Carson Valley, Chorpenning staked a quarter section of land and arranged to establish a mail station. The town of Genoa grew up around this site.[21]

However, Chorpenning was not the first to claim land in this area. In March of 1848, a group of Mormons coming from the Salt Lake Valley was heading for California. One in the group, H. S. Beatie, was taken with the beauty of the Carson Valley, and he took possession of a nearby site, and built a log cabin. Beatie would soon sell it to a man named Moore, who would then sell to John Reese in 1851. Reese's establishment would be known as Mormon Station from 1851 to 1857.

This became a popular supply station for emigrants and gold seekers traveling between Salt Lake City and California.

If Thompson and his half-brother came by way of the Carson River Route, they would have stopped there. Sometime, roughly around 1856-1857, when Brigham Young was calling all Mormons "home" to Salt Lake City because of the threat of the eminent "Mormon War," the name was changed from Mormon Station to Genoa.[22]

John Reese filed a claim in Justice Court of Carson Valley in the Utah Territory against Chorpenning for nonpayment for funds and supplies. It would appear from this claim that Chorpenning had been operating on credit from the beginning in 1851 and, therefore, was experiencing financial difficulties from the start.

Brief History of United States Mail on the California Trail

March 14, 1853

Application of John Reese for an attachment, To E. L. Barnard Justice of the Peace of Carson Valley, T.U.

The subscriber applies to you for an attachment against the property of G. Chorpenning Surviving Partner of Woodward and Co. on the grounds set forth hereunto annexed date as above.
John Reese one of the firm of Reese & Co. being duly sworn, says that Mr. George Chorpenning surviving partner of Woodward & Co. is justly indebted to this deponent and company in the sum of Six hundred and Seventy five dollars, over and above all discounts which the said Woodward & Co. or Chorpenning have or has against him or company as near as he can ascertain the same, which debt arose for funds and supplies furnished for them in transporting the mail from Salt Lake to Sacramento and back and that the said Chorpenning has departed from this valley and from California with the intent to defraud his creditors.
And his defendant further says, that unless he attaches the property now here he is afraid that he will

John A. "Snowshoe" Thompson
Pioneer Mail Carrier of the Sierra

forever lose the chance of collecting his demand.

Sworn to before me March 14, 1853
  E. L. Barnard
  Justice of the Peace

On March 16, 1853, Justice Barnard issued his decision:

Judgement [sic] is this day rendered in favor of the plaintiffs against the defendants before me Justice of the Peace for Seven Hundred Dollars damages and cost-Plaintiff appeared in Court defendant not present. Plaintiff swore to the correctness of his a/c Whereas I hereby award judgement .
E. L. Barnard J.P.
Damages $675.00
  Costs 25.00 March 16, 1853
    $700.00

On March 22, 1853,

  The amount of the execution levied of the goods and chattels of the defendant therein named.
  The within execution Satisfied in part to wit: for the sum of $519 and no goods or chattels of the defendants found whereof the residue could be made. Signed J. P. Barnard Const.

Brief History of United States Mail on the California Trail

One mule Sold to Reese	$91.
One do	$61 do
One do	$61 do
One do	$86 do
Compass chain etc.	$40
Smith tools Mormon Station	$130
	$519[23]

It is not clear if Chorpenning ever paid the remaining $181 of the $700 judgment. It is becoming clearer why Chorpenning may not have paid Snowshoe Thompson for his services, even though it would be three more years before Thompson would be hired by him to deliver mail in the winter. This pattern of financial difficulties burdened Chorpenning to the end of his mail delivery contracts, some six years later. Nonetheless, finances would not be the only trouble that would plague him.

The first year of Woodward and Chorpenning's mail delivery was fraught with problems, beginning with that sixteen-day journey over deep Sierra snow. Chorpenning finally made it to the Salt Lake Valley on June 5—taking over a month—which was a very long time considering pack animals carried the mail. Because mules carried the mail, it was soon known as "Jackass Mail."[24]

That first year of the contract there were winter snow problems, and during that first summer there were delays due to Indian problems, which affected Chorpenning's chances of fulfilling the

John A. "Snowshoe" Thompson
Pioneer Mail Carrier of the Sierra

mail contract schedule. In November, Woodward would not complete his eastward delivery, as he was attacked and killed by Indians in northern Utah.[25] The December and January mail runs were turned back by snow. This forced Chorpenning to seek an alternate route.

In February 1852, mail was sent by way of the Feather River Canyon and over Beckwourth Pass, which took sixty days to reach Salt Lake City. The men carried the mail on foot the last two hundred miles, because their animals froze to death near Goose Creek.[26] That was thirty days longer than the contract commitment.

Chorpenning, realizing that a Sierra winter crossing was not practical, sought and gained permission from the special agent in San Francisco, Mr. James Coggin, to send the March mail via a more southerly route. The plan was to dispatch the mail south by ship from San Francisco to San Pedro and then overland following the Mormon Trail (Old Spanish Trail) to Salt Lake Valley.[27]

Chorpenning continued to experience hardships, not only losing his partner at the hands of Indians, but losing animals and a number of employees, along with bags of mail—mail that never reached the easterly destinations. In 1852, the postmaster general, not being aware all of Chorpenning's difficulties, annulled Chorpenning's mail contract, and awarded the contract to W. L. Blanchard for a sum of $50,000.[28]

When he learned of the loss of his contract, Chorpenning set out for Washington D.C., with the intention of pleading his case.

Brief History of United States Mail on the California Trail

In the later part of January of 1853...I received notice that my contract had been annulled and awarded to W. L. Blanchard[29] *for $50,000 per annum for the same work... The contract required that Blanchard erect a fortified post in Carson Valley for the protection of the emigrants. This was so absurd to the settlers that it provoked frequent expressions of discussed [sic] on their part; for there had already been such a post there for nearly two years (Mormon Station) and besides that, the white population by this time in that vicinity out-numbered the Indian population greatly, and really left no need for such a post at all...*

Very soon after bringing my case before the department, it was proposed to reinstate me in my contract; but as my pay was inadequate, and as I had been let out of the matter honorably to myself, I refuse to go again without an increase in pay, and the right to claim damages for those sustained in breaking up my business.

It was finally agreed to, verbally, that I should have $16,000 per annum as additional compensation

---

* Ben Holiday was one of the sureties of Blanchard. Blanchard appealed to congress, an investigation was conducted, and Blanchard was awarded $22,916 in damages.

John A. "Snowshoe" Thompson
Pioneer Mail Carrier of the Sierra

> *for the balance of my contract term, and that I should be compensated for the extra work I had been doing. Whereupon the $50,000 contract was rescinded and on the 1st of July following (1853) I resumed work...** [30]

This was the beginning of a twenty-three-year battle between Chorpenning and the United States. Chorpenning would continue to tender the low bid to secure the contract, hoping for an adjusted compensation later.[31] However, his plan only worked to a point, as he always seemed to be facing financial difficulties, due to his heavy expenses and the constant slow payment by the government.

His most significant setback came in 1860 when the postmaster general annulled Chorpenning's contract for a third time. This time he would not be successful in reversing the decision, and the mail contract was awarded to William H. Russell.† [32]

After being awarded Chorpenning's mail delivery contract, Russell, along with Alexander Majors and William B. Waddell, bought up all available mail contracts. Russell, Majors, Waddell, and three other partners then held the contracts for the entire mail delivery service of the central route from the Missouri River to the Pacific Ocean.[33]

Does this event call into question any underhanded dealings, which resulted in

---

* Contract had to have been awarded to W. L. Blanchard.
† It is curious to note that in April of that same year, the Pony Express started its eighteen-month run, and was owned and operated by Russell, Majors, and Waddell. See Appendix F.

Brief History of United States Mail on the California Trail

Chorpenning being squeezed out of his mail contracts to make way for the powerful freighting company of Russell, Majors and Waddell?

The effects of this transaction must have also had an impact on Thompson's mail delivery position. An attempt to sort out Thompson's situation will be made later in this study. Nevertheless, it has become clearer that with all of Chorpenning's financial difficulties, he was not able to pay Thompson for his mail delivery services. Chorpenning was out of business and in debt. Thompson was out of luck regarding any pay due him.

John A. "Snowshoe" Thompson
Pioneer Mail Carrier of the Sierra

5

John Thompson Delivers the Mail

The details of Thompson being hired to carry the mail in the winter are described here as cited from the Carson Valley Historical Society publication, *Snowshoe Thompson: His Life and Adventures.*[1]

> Once Thompson felt competent enough to cope with any situation that might arise if he carried the mail to Genoa, he approached the Placerville postmaster, Mr. Thatcher, to apply for the job. When Thompson arrived at the post office, Thatcher saw standing before him a young man with piercing blue eyes, fair hair, a straight back and a muscular physique. Thompson was six feet tall, thin, wiry and weighed, perhaps 160 pounds.

JOHN THOMPSON DELIVERS THE MAIL

Original Placerville Post Office Site
Photo by Author

Thatcher proceeded to tell Thompson a little bit about the dangers awaiting a person foolish enough to attempt crossing the mountains during the winter.

Thatcher told him about two men, Chorpenning and Woodward, who took a mail contract in 1851. It took them 16 days of incredible hardship to cross the mountains and their horses froze to death in the bitter cold. He also mentioned two men, Bishop and Dritt who had alternated in trips across the mountains in the spring of 1853. A man named George

John A. "Snowshoe" Thompson
Pioneer Mail Carrier of the Sierra

Pierce had succeeded them, followed by Jack C. Johnson. These men all used the Canadian type of snowshoe and found the trip too slow and dangerous. Thatcher told Thompson it is impossible to keep on course when you are trapped in a massive windstorm or snow storm such as often raged in the mountains.

Thompson then described the snowshoes he planned to use which were quite different from anything seen before in the area.... Thompson went on to explain to Thatcher that he could follow trees and rocks during the day and he could use the stars at night as his guide.

After Thompson explained this, Thatcher extended his hand as a gesture of confirmation and said: "The people of Utah will certainly be glad to hear about you. They are the ones petitioning the government for something to be done about being snowed in for six months of the year. So, Mr. Thompson, you have to see the postmaster at Genoa about your pay."*

---

* Could this be a clue to the typical government "run around" on who was responsible for paying Thompson?

JOHN THOMPSON DELIVERS THE MAIL

The arrangements for Thompson being hired to carry the mail are still not clear—neither the amount of pay Thompson was to receive, nor how often he was contracted to deliver the mail between Placerville and the Carson Valley in the Utah Territory. "Thompson had started to carry the mail for $1 per letter; but often he could not collect it from the addressees."[2]

Just who was Thompson working for—the Post Office Department, or George Chorpenning? It has always been assumed that it was George Chorpenning, the holder of the contract to deliver the mail between San Francisco and Salt Lake City. Nonetheless, it was documented that Thompson's first mail delivery was in January of 1856, with this account that appeared in the *Sacramento Union*, dated January 19 of that year.

> *Mr. John A. Thompson, who resides on Putah Creek, in Yolo County, left Carson Valley on Tuesday morning last, and reached this city at noon yesterday. Mr. T. is engaged in conveying an express to and fro from 'the Valley.'*
>
> *About last December, Elder Orson Hyde, of the Mormon sect, together with a man named Willis, started to cross the mountains on horseback. They had proceeded as far*

John A. "Snowshoe" Thompson
Pioneer Mail Carrier of the Sierra

as the second summit* when the snow got so deep that Willis took the horses and returned. Elder Hyde started to come through on foot, and had reached a point within three miles of Slippery Ford† when he retraced his steps, but before he arrived at Carson Valley, had both of his feet frozen.

Meantime, Willis and the two horses have not been heard of, and it is naturally supposed that he became bewildered, benumbed, and finally froze to death.

On the night of December 24th, some person or persons broke into the store of Mr. Job, about ten miles above Mormon Station, and stole therefrom one thousand dollars worth of goods. No clue to the whereabouts of the thief has been found.

Mr. Thompson was three days and a half incoming through from Carson Valley, and used on the snow the Norwegian skates, which are manufactured of wood, and some seven feet in length. He furthermore states that he found the snow about five-feet deep between Slippery Ford

---

* This would appear to be Johnson Pass, near today's Echo Summit on U.S. 50. The first summit would have been either Luther Pass, CA SR 89, or Daggett Pass, Nevada State Route 207. When coming west from Carson Valley, Echo Summit would be the second summit.

† Near present day town of Strawberry, U.S. 50.

John Thompson Delivers the Mail

and the summit,* a distance of eight miles, and on the average elsewhere in the mountains, three feet deep.

Mr. Bishop, who carried over the Salt Lake mail in December, consumed eight days in crossing, and before getting through, was badly frozen.

Mr. Thompson left Placerville for Carson Valley on January 3d, and leaves again on his trans-mountain trip this day.

The fact that Thompson was able to deliver the mail over the deep snow of these high mountains, and in such a short period of time, was big news. Earlier attempts to carry the mail in the winter had been disasters, as described by what Hyde and Willis experienced.

Sacramento Union, *February 4, 1856:*

The adventurous and hardy mountain expressman, Mr. John A. Thompson, again arrived in this city on yesterday, from Carson Valley, bringing us a fortnight's later intelligence. Mr. T. left this city on the outward trip on the 19th, and arrived in the Valley in five days thereafter, having encountered few difficulties of moment.

---

* This would be Johnson Pass near today's Echo Summit.

John A. "Snowshoe" Thompson
Pioneer Mail Carrier of the Sierra

He set out on his return journey at meridian[3] *on Wednesday of the last week, taking his departure from the foot of Daggett's Cut-off, three miles above Mormon Station. The perilous passage of this almost precipitous pass was made in safety, and our hero arrived by nightfall at Kelly & Roger's Inn, situated on the beach of Lake Bigler* [Lake Tahoe]. *These enterprising fellows have erected a comfortable house, and are in snug winter quarters...*

On the evening of the second day our informant succeeded in reaching Slippery Ford, but had a seven day's tramp on his Norwegian skates. On the summit, and thence down to the Ford, he found the snow seven feet deep. Its average depth along the route was from four to seven feet.

Two men started on snow shoes with Mr. Thompson and accompanied him as far as the Summit [Johnson Pass], *but at that point "turned back and walked no more with him."*

---

* "In January 1856 the inhabitants of Carson Valley again petitioned the California Legislature to annex them for judicial and other purposes. A resolution passed in that body asking congress to make the 118 meridian the east boundary of California."

JOHN THOMPSON DELIVERS THE MAIL

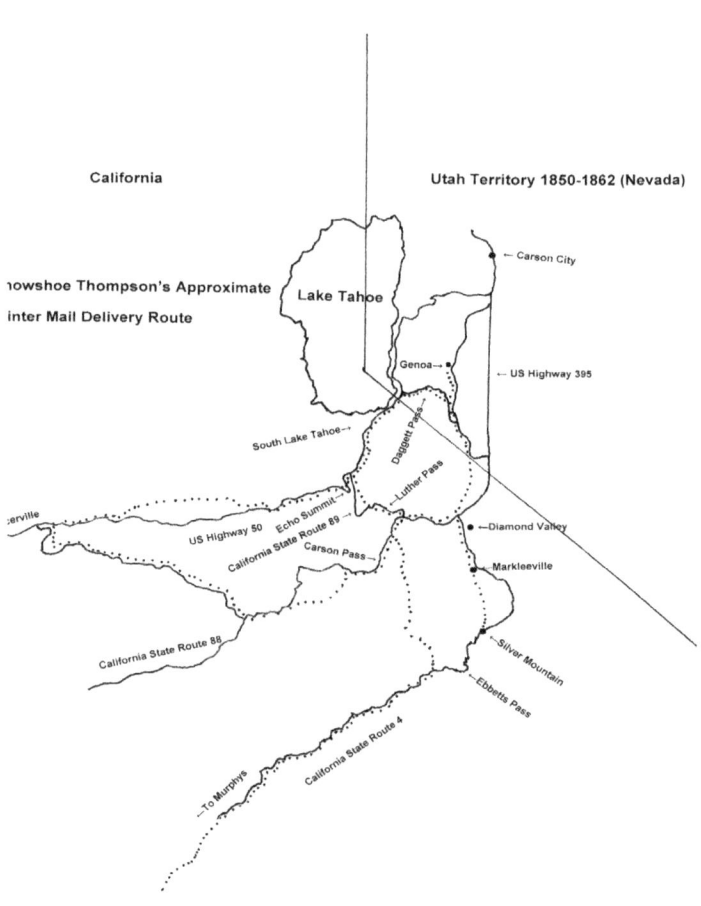

Map of Thompson's Approximate Winter Delivery Route
Photo by Author

John A. "Snowshoe" Thompson
Pioneer Mail Carrier of the Sierra

On the third day Mr. Thompson came as far as Brocklis' [sic] trading post... *On Saturday evening our mountain expressman arrived in Placerville, having traveled forty-five miles on snow shoes, and the entire distance between the termini...*

Brother Orson Hyde was at Mormon Station, and nearly recovered from the serious frost biting he got in the mountains. The people there are anxious to learn the fate of the petition forwarded to the legislature, praying the annexation of the Valley to this State and also as to the fate of the wagon road.[†][4]

There has been no communication for some time with Salt Lake owing to the heavy snows on the Goose Creek Mountains, and the scarcity of provisions for animals along the route. The latest news from Deseret[‡] *was brought to them by Mr. Thompson on his last* transmontane *tour. He leaves*

---

* Brockliss trading post was located approximately twenty-two miles east of Placerville on the bank of the American River near U.S. 50.

† In 1855, the California legislature directed the state surveyor to investigate the existing wagon trails with the possibility of building a single commercial wagon road over the Sierra into Carson Valley and a possible route for the transcontinental railroad.

‡ Brigham Young suggested this name for the state that became known as Utah.

JOHN THOMPSON DELIVERS THE MAIL

again on Wednesday next, and any letters or papers to be forwarded by him should be left at the St. Charles Hotel, on I street, and in Placerville at the Placer Hotel.

No one knows the exact route Thompson traveled during his mail runs across the Sierra, but there are many clues as to the general route. In the previous article, there are place names such as Daggett's, Lake Valley (South Lake Tahoe), Slippery Ford, and Brockliss trading post, all located along established wagon routes. Homes, ranches, and businesses were established, so it is likely that Thompson knew the people along the route. He would have passed their way, possibly delivering mail and other items they requested.

In Francis P. Farquhar's Sierra Nevada study, he described Thompson's route: "...At first he used the Placerville-Johnson-Luther Pass route, but later the Big Tree route to Hope Valley, where both routes continued down the Carson Canyon to Genoa."[5]

Generally, Thompson was thought to have followed along Johnson Cutoff, established in 1852.[6] This is the approximate route of modern day U.S. 50 from Placerville to Lake Tahoe,* and beyond. The

---

*John Calhoun Johnson, Sierra explorer and founder of "Johnson Cutoff" (now U.S. 50), named the lake "Lake Bigler" in honor of John Bigler, California's third governor. In 1853, William Eddy, the surveyor general of California, identified Tahoe as Lake Bigler. In 1862, the U.S. Department of the Interior first introduced the name Tahoe. Both names were used until well into the next century. The lake did not receive its official and final designation as Lake Tahoe until 1945.

John A. "Snowshoe" Thompson
Pioneer Mail Carrier of the Sierra

land around the south end of Lake Bigler (Lake Tahoe) was usually referred to as Lake Valley during the time Thompson was delivering mail.

Present day U.S. 50 closely follows the South Fork of the American River, but the early wagon road travelers stayed on the ridge tops whenever a river canyon became steep and narrow.

Peavine Ridge is one such location and it is most likely where Thompson would have chosen to travel. Slippery Ford is near Strawberry, California, and east of Peavine Ridge; Johnson Pass is just north of present day Echo Summit.

After Thompson dropped down into Lake Valley, he had two choices: One route was over Daggett Pass, elevation 7,344 feet, from Lake Valley and down present-day Kingsbury Grade[7] to Carson Valley and Mormon Station. The other route was Luther Pass* to Hope Valley, down the Woodfords Canyon, then to Carson Canyon, and on to Mormon Station. With so much snow on the ground, Thompson did not need to travel the exact location of the wagon roads. It seems logical and practical that he would have taken the route of least resistance, the most trouble-free, and most direct routes as possible.

Thompson continued to make the news as is revealed in this article from the *Sacramento Union*, dated December 10, 1856:

> *Mr. J. A. Thompson, the Carson Valley Expressman called upon us yesterday, having made his first trip of this year*

---
* Luther Pass is a section of CA SR 89 that connects U.S. 50 with CA SR 88 in Hope Valley.

JOHN THOMPSON DELIVERS THE MAIL

from the valley. The journey was as usual, in winter, performed on foot. He left Carson Valley on Thursday, Dec. 4^{th,} and reached Placerville on Monday Dec. 8th.

On Thursday night, Mr. Thompson stopped at the cabin of "Uncle Billy Rogers" in Hope Valley.*

In Carson Valley, when Mr. Thompson left, there was about four inches of snow, and on the summit of the Sierras [sic], for a distance of about thirty miles, there was a depth of three feet. For twenty miles more on this slope, the snow was about a foot and a half...

The Mormons and the Gentiles in the Valley are just now at peace, although the boundary line question still excites a good deal of interest. The Mormons want the Valley in Utah—the Gentiles, in California. The Utah and the California assessors have both assessed the property, and the consequence is that the owners will not pay taxes to either.

Mr. Thompson says that if by next season something is not done by Sacramento and Placerville towards the opening of the road by way of Johnson's Cutoff, the travel will go by

---
* The Rogers cabin was located near Red Lake. Thompson was following the Carson River Route. See Appendix H.

John A. "Snowshoe" Thompson
Pioneer Mail Carrier of the Sierra

the way of Murphy's. Mr. Thompson came by way of the Old Carson road.

Thompson was relating some of the political unrest of the wagon road issue. In 1852, the Johnson, Beckwourth, Nobles, Henness, and Sonora routes were added to the Truckee and Carson routes for wagon travel.[8]

By 1856, the competition was great to lure pioneers and gold seekers to numerous other areas of California by way of the newer wagon roads. The plan was to siphon wagon train and mule team traffic from the major routes onto their roads and their respective businesses where people would spend their money.

The events of that first year, 1856, when Thompson delivered mail, would define Thompson's place in history.

The detailed article in the *Sacramento Union*, dated January 10, 1857, best explains this next event:

> *J. A. Thompson, the expressman of the Sierra Nevada Mountains* [sic], *called upon us yesterday upon completion of his second trip this winter to Carson Valley, and placed us in possession of some highly interesting particulars connected therewith. This trip is particularly interesting from the fact that it was made on his Norwegian snow shoes, seven and a half feet long, over snow which, at some points, he was unable to fathom.*

John Thompson Delivers the Mail

About three miles above Placerville, he came to the snow, having left this place on the 20th of December. He was accompanied by two men who had waited his going, and at this point they all put on their snow shoes. The weather was clear, but cold and the party made Lake Valley without any incident worth note.

On the night of the 23d of December, they reached a deserted cabin in that valley and struck a fire. Mr. Thompson being anxious to press on, told his companions that he would go ahead and stay overnight at another cabin about a mile ahead, and they could overtake him in the morning. Although anxious to stop, rather than separate from him, they determined to go on that night, and once more they all started off.

About midnight, they reached the cabin, and found everything dark, and the door closed. Mr. Thompson—not expecting to find any one in—however, knocked and 'hallooed' when to his surprise a voice answered from within. On entering, Mr. Thompson found a man lying alone upon the floor in that dreary spot, without other covering than the cloths he wore, and boots frozen to his feet. In this deplorable condition he

John A. "Snowshoe" Thompson
Pioneer Mail Carrier of the Sierra

had been lying for twelve days, with nothing to sustain life but raw flour. His feet were completely frozen, and will both have to be amputated below the knee.

His suffering must, according to the statement of Mr. Thompson, have been indescribable, and yet he bore them with fortitude of a martyr, and scarcely permitted a murmur to escape him. Although death would soon have terminated his agony, he still had a lingering hope that Providence might direct Mr. Thompson by his cabin, and thus save him. Had not Mr. T. gone on that night he would probably have passed the cabin in the morning without stopping.

The sufferer proved to be James Sisson, the partner of Mr. [Asa] Hawley, about six miles above Placerville. He had been engaged in the packing business, and left for Carson Valley on snowshoes some two weeks previous. The storm overtook him on his way, and his feet becoming frozen, it was with great difficulty he reached his cabin or trading post. On arriving there he found his matches so wet he could not strike a light, and thus he remained for four days, when he discovered a box of matches in his cabin which furnished him with fire.

John Thompson Delivers the Mail

> He then attempted to cut his boots off his feet, but could not succeed, and nothing remained for him but to await either a succor or death.
>
> On the 24th, Mr. Thompson started for Carson Valley, and on Christmas day got five men to agree to accompany him back to Lake Valley. He rigged them out with snow shoes, made after the pattern of his own, and taking with them a sled upon which to haul the sufferer, they started back on the 26th.
>
> They reached the trading post that night, and laid over during the 27th, in consequences of the severe weather—another snow being falling. On the 28th, they packed Mr. Sisson on the sled, and thus, with great labor, succeeded in conveying him safely to Carson Valley, where the sufferer is now laying in the camp of Dr. Daggett. Mr. Thompson, on his return will take with him some chloroform which will be administered to the patient and his feet amputated—as it was not deemed advisable to attempt the operation without this agency.

Dan De Quille's version of this story adds some further details of interest to the event:

John A. "Snowshoe" Thompson
Pioneer Mail Carrier of the Sierra

About Christmas, in the year 1856, Snow-Shoe Thompson saved the life of James Sisson, who had been lying in an old deserted cabin in Lake Valley for twelve days with his feet frozen. There was some flour in the cabin, and on this Sisson had subsisted. He was in the cabin for four days without a fire. During this time he ate the flour raw, just as it came out of the sack.

On the fifth day, while rummaging about the cabin, he had good fortune to find some matches. These were where no one would have thought of looking for matches, as they were scattered about under some hay that lay on the floor. After finding the matches, Sisson made a fire and thawed out his boots, when he was able to get them off. For four days he had lain in the cabin with his boots frozen to his feet.

When found by Mr. Thompson, eight days later, Sisson's legs were purple to the knees. Sisson was confident from the appearance of his legs that mortification had set in. He knew unless his legs were amputated, he must soon die. As he could expect no assistance from the outside world, he concluded to himself undertake to perform the required operation.

John Thompson Delivers the Mail

There was an ax in the cabin, and with this he was determined to cut off his frozen legs. But for the opportune arrival of Thompson, Sisson would the next day have attempted to disjoint his legs at the knees; for that was the day he had fixed upon for undertaking the operation.

At the time he found Sisson, Thompson was on his way from Placerville to Carson. It was in the night, and coming to the log house, which was occupied in the summer as a trading post, Thomson halted for a moment, and was knocking the snow off his shoes by striking them against cabin, when he heard some one cry out. Going inside, he found Sisson situated as he related above. A considerable amount of provisions had been left in cabin in the fall, but all except the flour had been stolen by the Indians.

Thompson chopped a supply of wood for the unfortunate man, and making him as comfortable as was possible with the means at hand, left for Genoa to obtain assistance. While Thompson was cutting the wood, Sisson called out to him and begged him not to dull the ax—the place being full of rocks—as he might yet want it for the purpose of taking off his legs.

Sisson was firmly of the opinion

John A. "Snowshoe" Thompson
Pioneer Mail Carrier of the Sierra

that when Thompson left him he would never see him again. He thought Thompson would never be able to get down out of the mountains, and was of the opinion that in case he did succeed in reaching the valley, he would not attempt to return to the cabin.

Mr. Thompson told Sisson he would surely return and take him away, and advised him not to think of attempting to amputate his legs, as on cutting the arteries he would bleed to death. But Sisson had thought of that.

He intended to make a sort of compress or tourniquet of some pieces of baling-rope, which he would twist around his legs with a stick, in such a way that a bit of rock would be pressed upon the arteries. Then with fire-brands he would sear the ends of the arteries, and the raw flesh of the stumps of his legs.

Sisson's mind was so much occupied with the plans of amputation of his legs, that Thompson was afraid to leave the ax where he could get hold of it: he did so only upon receiving from Sisson a solemn promise that he would wait three days before attempting to use it on his knees.

On leaving the cabin, Thompson traveled all night, and early

John Thompson Delivers the Mail

the next morning arrived at Genoa. Here he raised a party of six men. By Thompson's advice the party carried with them a few tools for making a sled. Snow-shoes were hastily constructed for the men composing the relief party. As none of these men had ever done much traveling on snow-shoes, they furnished Thompson not a little amusement during the journey, by their mishaps and involuntary antics.

After much hard work, the party arrived at the lone cabin late in the evening, to the great joy of Sisson, who at sight of so many men felt that he was saved.

That night they constructed a hand-sled on which to carry the frozen man down to Carson Valley. In the morning they awoke to find that nearly two feet of new snow had fallen; there was a depth of eight feet before. The new snow made it very hard to get along with the hand-sled. Under Sisson's weight it plowed deeply along, and at times buried almost out of sight.

The first day the party got no farther than Hope Valley, where they encamped. Sisson was made as comfortable as possible on a bed of boughs. As they had expected to reach Genoa in one day, they had taken

John A. "Snowshoe" Thompson
Pioneer Mail Carrier of the Sierra

along with them no blankets, and but few other comforts, for the frozen man.

The second day they reached Genoa, and at once procured the medical assistance which Sisson's case so urgently demanded. The doctors found that it be necessary to amputate both of Sisson's feet. Before the operation could be performed, however, the physician said he must have some chloroform.

As Snow-shoe Thompson never did things by halves, he at once set out, crossed the Sierra, and traveled all the way to Sacramento, in order to get the required drug. Finally, the long-delayed operation was performed. Sisson survived, and at last accounts, was living in the Atlantic States.[9]

Both accounts boggle the mind. The *Sacramento Union* article listed the time line details:

- December 10—Thompson left Placerville with two other men.
- December 23—arrived in Lake Valley and found Sisson in a cabin
- December 24—left Sisson and departed for Genoa
- December 25—reached Genoa

JOHN THOMPSON DELIVERS THE MAIL

- December 27—arrived back at Lake Valley with a rescue party
- December 28—left Lake Valley with Sisson
- December 29—reached Genoa, having to overnight in Hope Valley due to a storm
- Date uncertain—Thompson headed for Placerville, then Sacramento for chloroform, and returned to Genoa in time to save Sisson's life.[*]
- January 9—Thompson arrived back in Placerville, reporting to the newspaper the next day.

During this twenty-day adventure, Thompson covered some four hundred or more miles to deliver the mail and save a man's life. This was huge news, and it established John "Snowshoe" Thompson's place in history and legend.

Many poems and songs were written about Snowshoe Thompson, such as this, written by W. F. Skyhawk:[10] Pony Express Historical Series No. 17.[11]

---

[*] The research does not report how long it took Thompson to travel to Sacramento and back to Genoa.

John A. "Snowshoe" Thompson
Pioneer Mail Carrier of the Sierra

Down Genoa's Peak Descending
(Snow Shoe Thomson Brings Chloroform)

Flying Eagle of the Fifties
Soaring Bird Man of the West
Sailing through the virgin forest,
Scaling, high, Sierra's crest.

Down Genoa's Peak descending;
'Round the crags, and 'tween the pine.
Clouds of snow, like smoking engines,
Trailing in the serpentine.

"Down! Down! Fast there comes a-falling
Like a streak of lightning's ray—
Swinging, bending, leaping, swirling,
See the comet wend its way!

"Hail, ye Mormon Saints and Gentiles!
Elzy Knott shut down your mill!
Snow Shoe Thomson! Ho! He's coming!
Sisson's legs will soon be nil.

"Daggett, Chamberlain and Waters,
Chloroform is on the way!
Get your cleavers, saws and cat-gut!
Go to work and save the day!

Sisson's ends are mortifying,
Thirty days they're frozen stiff!
Doctor Luce, with Pony whiskey.
Take your turn at every sniff!"

6

"Snowshoe" the Man

From the previous chapter Thompson appeared to have great endurance and strength beyond most men. He never seemed to suffer from the cold as did so many others.

Dan De Quille wrote of Snowshoe Thompson just three months before the legend's death.

> *Mr. Thompson was a man of splendid physique, standing six feet tall in stocking feet, and weighing 180 pounds. His features were large, but regular and handsome. He had blond hair and beard, and fair skin and blue eyes of his Scandinavian ancestors; and looked a true descendant of a sea-roving Northman of old. Although he spoke English as well as a native born American, one would not have been much surprised to have heard him break forth in the old Norse.... His frame muscular and his* tout ensemble

John A. "Snowshoe" Thompson
Pioneer Mail Carrier of the Sierra

> *that of a hardy mountaineer... His face wore that aspect of repose, and he had that calmness of manner, which are a result of perfect self-reliance.*

De Quille once asked Thompson if he ever got lost.

> *"No" he said, "I was never lost—I can't be lost! I can go anywhere in the mountains, day or night, storm or shine. I can't be lost," repeated he, tapping his forehead with his forefinger.*
> *"I've got something in here that keeps me right. I have found many persons who were lost—dozens of men, first and last—but never been lost myself. There is no danger of getting lost in a narrow range of mountains like the Sierras [sic], if a man has his wits about him."*

De Quille's biography of Thompson, "The Skiing Mailman of the Sierra" appeared in the October 1886 issue of the *Overland Monthly.*

As previously stated, De Quille derived much of his information from the one interview with Thompson, and he acknowledged that his other information was acquired from letters written to those mountain men who knew Thompson.[1]

Following is a segment of De Quille's writings of Thompson's skill, dedication, dependability, and amazing adventures.

"Snowshoe" the Man

While traveling in the mountains, Snow-shoe Thompson never carried blankets, nor did he even wear an overcoat. The weight and bulk of such articles would have encumbered and discommoded him. Exercise kept him warm while traveling, and when he encamped he always built a fire. He carried as little as possible besides the bags containing the mail. During the first year or two after he went into the business, he carried a revolver. Finding, however, that he had no use for such a weapon, and being of the first importance to travel as light as possible, he presently concluded to leave his pistol at home.

All that he carried in way of provisions was a small quantity of jerked beef, or dried sausage, and a few crackers or biscuits. He never carried provisions that need to be cooked. For drink he caught a handful of snow or lay down for a moment and quaffed the water of some stream or brook. He never took with him brandy, whisky, or liquor of any kind. He was a man that seldom tasted liquor.

Snow-shoe never stopped for storms. He always set out on the day appointed, without regard to the

John A. "Snowshoe" Thompson
Pioneer Mail Carrier of the Sierra

weather, and he traveled by night as well as in the daytime. He pursued no regular path—in a trackless waste of snow there was no path to follow—but kept to a general route or course. By day he was guided by the trees and rocks, and by night looked to the stars, as a mariner to his compass. With the places of many stars he was familiar as ever as was Hansteen,* ² the great astronomer [and physicist] of the land of his birth.

At the time Thompson began snow-shoeing in the Sierras [sic], nothing was known of the mysteries of "dope"—a preparation of pitch, tallow, and other ingredients, which, being applied to the bottom of the shoes enables the wearer to lightly glide over snow softened by the rays of the sun. Dope appears to have been a California discovery. It is made of different qualities, and different degree of hardness and softness. Each California snow-shoe runner has his "dope secret" or his "pet" dope, and some are so nice in this respect as to carry with them dope for different hours of the day; using one quality in the morning, when the snow is

---
* Christopher Hansteen, a Norwegian, born September 26, 1784, Christiania (now Oslo), Norway, died April 15, 1873.

"Snowshoe" the Man

frozen, and others later on, as the snow becomes soft.*

As Thompson used no dope, soft snow stuck to and so clogged his shoes that it was sometimes impossible for him to travel over it. Thus, it frequently happened the he was obliged to halt for several hours during the day, and resume his journey at night, when the crust was frozen on the snow's night camps—whenever the night was such as prevented him from continuing his journey, or when it was necessary for him to obtain sleep—were generally made wherever he happened to be at the moment. He did not push forward to reach particular points, as springs or brooks. He was always able to substitute snow for water, without feeling any bad effect.

He always tried, however, to find the stump of a dead pine, at which to make his camp. After setting fire to the dry stump, he collected a quantity of fir or spruce boughs, with which he constructed a sort of rude couch or platform on the snow. Stretched upon his bed of boughs, with his feet to the fire, and his head resting upon one of his Uncle Sam's mail bags, he slept as soundly as if occupying the best bed

---

* See La Porte boy's ski dope, Chapter 8.

John A. "Snowshoe" Thompson
Pioneer Mail Carrier of the Sierra

ever made; though perhaps, beneath his couch there was depth of from ten to twenty feet of snow.

Occasionally, his slumbers were interrupted by either disagreeable or startling accidents. Sometimes his fire, burning downward toward the roots of the stub or stump beside which he camped, melted the snow under his platform of boughs to such an extent that it was undermined, and then he suddenly found himself sliding down into a deep pit—a pit filled with fire.
When unable to find a dry stump, he looked for a dead pine tree. He always selected a tree that had to it a decided lean. If he could avoid it, he never made his camp beside a tree that was perfectly straight. For this there was a good reason. It very often happened that the tree set on fire in the evening was burned through, and fell to the ground before morning. When he had a leaning tree, at the foot of which to encamp, he was able to make his bed on the safe side...

The CVHS publication on Thompson described his travels thus:

"Snowshoe" the Man

> Snowshoe managed to climb mountains by zigzagging. Keeping his skis at just enough angle to prevent him from sliding backwards. Once he reached a ridge he tried to stay there because every downhill schuss simply meant he would have to climb uphill again.
> Quite often a blizzard would be raging in the mountains, which was so severe it was impossible for him to proceed. He knew he could not lie down or he would be buried in the snow and freeze to death. When confronted by such a storm, Snowshoe would find a flat rock large enough to stand on then he would dance Norwegian folk dances until the snow subsided.[3]

De Quille's biography of Thompson continued:

> However, he did not always camp by trees and stumps. Sometimes, he crawled under shelving rocks, and there made his bed of boughs, building a fire on bare ground in front of it. At a place called Cottage Rock, six miles below Strawberry Valley, he had a small, dry cavern, in the shape of an oven, in which he was in the habit of housing, as often as he could make it convenient to do so.[4]

John A. "Snowshoe" Thompson
Pioneer Mail Carrier of the Sierra

Local legend claims another similar place to Cottage Rock, called "Snowshoe Thompson Cave." It consists of overhanging granite boulders and is located in the canyon where the West Fork of the Carson River flows east from Hope Valley into Carson Valley.

It has all the characteristics as described for Cottage Rock and would make a good shelter. It does raise a question regarding Thompson's use of this cave, however, mainly due to its location to Woodfords, which is only about four miles downhill from the cave, near the mouth of the canyon. In most seasons, there would not be a lot of snow that would last all winter at Woodfords' elevation of 5,617 feet.

Cottage Rock
Courtesy: El Dorado County Historical Museum

"Snowshoe" the Man

Snowshoe Thompson Cave   *Photo by Author*

The cave is about two miles east of the junction of CA SR 88 and 89, in Hope Valley on Carson River Route of the California Trail.[5]

Thompson probably would not have used this cave going east, unless there was a storm so great that he could not go any farther. It would have been an incredible coincidence for him to run out of visibility at the same time he arrived at the cave. On the other hand, if he was going west and having trouble seeing because of darkness or a snow whiteout, it would have been the perfect place for Thompson to find shelter and wait out a storm. Unfortunately, Snowshoe's use of this "cave" sometime during his twenty years of delivering the mail is supported only by local oral history.

JOHN A. "SNOWSHOE" THOMPSON
PIONEER MAIL CARRIER OF THE SIERRA

Dan De Quille described Thompson's experience with bears, which was only one of two stories written of his encountering wild animals during his mail delivering duties.

> Although Snowshoe Thompson traveled about the wilds of the Sierra for more than twenty winters, he never in all that time encountered a grizzly bear, or even saw a bear of any kind. Hundreds of times, however, he saw their tracks in the snow, and also in the mud about springs and brooks. Sometimes the tracks he saw had been so recently made that the water from the oozy ground was still running into and had not filled them.
>
> At times he was so close upon them that he imagined their odor still lingering in the air. Not infrequently he came to places where a number of bears had been traveling together. He once saw where a troop of eight had passed along. He several times saw the track of a huge grizzly with a club-foot, known to the mountain men and hunters as "Old Brin," a name given to the beast on account of his being of a peculiar brindle color. When he had a clear field, Thompson did not fear the bears; he could easily run away from them on his snow-shoes.[6]

"Snowshoe" the Man

De Quille used Thompson's own words regarding the second story of his encounters with wild animals.

> *I was never frightened but once during my travels in the mountains. That was the winter of 1857. I was crossing Hope Valley, when I came to a place where six great wolves—big timber wolves—were at work in the snow, digging out the carcass of some animal. Now, in my childhood, in Norway, I had heard so many stories of the ferocity of wolves, that I feared them more than any other wild animal. To my eyes, those before me looked to have hair on them a foot long.*
>
> *They were great gaunt, shaggy fellows. My course lay near them. I knew I must show a bold front. All my life I had heard that the wolf, savage and cruel as he is, seldom has the courage to attack anything that does not run at his approach. I might easily run away from bears, but these are customers of a different kind. There was nothing of them but bones, sinews, and hair. They could skim over the snow like birds.*
>
> *As I approached, the wolves left the carcass, and in single file came out a distance of about twenty five yards toward my line of march. The leader of*

John A. "Snowshoe" Thompson
Pioneer Mail Carrier of the Sierra

the pack then wheeled around and sat down on his haunches. When the next one came up he did the same thing, and so on until all were seated in a line. They acted just like trained soldiers. I pledge you my word, I thought the devil was in them!

There they sat, every eye and every sharp nose turned toward me as I approached. In the old-country I had heard of "man-wolves," and these acted as if of that supernatural kind. To look at them gave me cold chills, and I had a queer feeling about the roots of my hair. What most frightened me was the confidence they displayed, and the regular order in which they moved. But I dared not show the least sign of fear, so on I went.

Just when I was opposite them, and but twenty five or thirty yards away, the leader of the pack threw back his heard, and uttered a loud and prolonged howl. All the others of the pack did the same. Ya-hoo-oo, woo-oo! cried all together. A more doleful and terrific sound I never heard.

I thought it meant my death. The awful cry rang across the silent valley, was echoed by the hills, and re-echoed far away among the surrounding ridges. Every moment I expected to see the whole pack dash at *me. I would just then have given all I possessed to have had my revolver in my hand.*

However, I did not alter my gait nor change my line of march. I passed the file of wolves as a general moves along in front of his soldiers. The ugly brutes uttered but their first fearful howl. When they saw that their war cry didn't cause me to alter my course nor make me run they feared to come after me; so they let me pass.

They sat still and watched hungrily for some time, but when I was far away I saw them all turn about and go back to the carcass. Had I turned back, or tried to run away, when they marched out to meet me, I'm confident the whole pack would have been upon me in a moment. They all looked it. My show of courage intimidated them, and kept them back.[7]

Thompson was notably civic minded and always ready to be of help to people and to his community. For example, Thompson worked with Thomas Knott to build a sawmill and gristmill in Carson Valley. He helped the Peter Vallem family raise a barn. Vallem was a Norwegian who migrated from Norway in 1856. Thompson also served as a witness when Vallem filed his naturalization papers.[8]

He seemed to volunteer for whatever job was needed as illustrated in this article that appeared in

John A. "Snowshoe" Thompson
Pioneer Mail Carrier of the Sierra

the *San Andreas Independent,* dated May 1, 1858:
1857: A Good Appointment

> *Our readers will be gratified to learn that Major Dodge has appointed J. A. Thompson sub-agent among the Indians on Walker's river.* Thompson is the pioneer expressman who traveled the passes of the Sierra Nevada on foot, summer and winter, rain or shine, three years ago, bringing and taking whatever letters or news astir on either side of the mountain. He is a brave, thought-going, honest-hearted man, and will doubtless look closely after the affairs of the poor savages with whom he has been appointed to reside.*

An almost duplicate article appeared on July 7, 1860, over two years later in the same newspaper, announcing the same appointment in similar wording:

> *Thompson, J. A. Appointed Indian Agent 1857: A Good Appointment. Our readers will be gratified to learn that Major Dodge has appointed J. A. Thompson sub-agent among the Indians on Walker's river. Thompson is the pioneer expressman who traveled*

---
* This was the Paiute Indian Tribe. On November 29, 1859, the Walker River Paiute Indian Reservation was established.

"SNOWSHOE" THE MAN

the passes of the Sierra Nevada on foot, summer and winter, rain or snow, three years ago, bringing and taking whatever letters were then astir on either side of the mountains. He is a brave, thought-going, honest-hearted man, and will doubtless look closely after the affairs of the poor savages amongst whom he has been appointed to reside.

This duplication of the article could be an indication of how popular Snowshoe Thompson was to journalists and readers alike.

Utah Territorial Governor, Alfred Cumming,*[9] appointed Thompson as Notary Public in 1859.

Documentation of his dealings with Indians are scarce, but this one civic service activity almost ended the life and story of John A. Thompson. It had to have had a profound effect on him. It was a major encounter with Paiute Indians that came to be known as the "Paiute War of 1860," or "Pyramid Lake War."

Many accounts of the war usually gloss it over as a minor incident. However, as documented here, it is shown to be a major event in history of northwestern Nevada. When this war occurred, Nevada was still part of the Utah Territory.

It is difficult to pinpoint when the first event occurred and exactly which event lead up to the "Paiute War of 1860." Strained relationships between

---

* Cumming accepted President James Buchanan's appointment as Governor of Utah Territory in July of 1857, replacing Brigham Young. He arrived in Salt Lake on April 12, 1858.

John A. "Snowshoe" Thompson
Pioneer Mail Carrier of the Sierra

Indians and whites had been going on for years in the Midwest and in the East. In California, the unrest between Indians and whites can be traced as far back as the first Spanish invasion of California in 1769 with the Portola expedition, or possibly with even earlier explorers.

There was an extensive trading exchange between the California Indians and the Great Basin Indians. Indians on the east side of the Sierra Nevada were getting information on how the Spaniards were treating Indians in California. It is only natural that the Great Basin Indians would become leery of the white man.

Most likely, many of those early parties coming through the area might have frightened the Indians living along the Mary's River. It would make sense that stories, or dire warnings, concerning these strange people would have traveled quickly among the various tribes.

Peter Skeen Ogden and his trapping party came into this unnamed river country in 1829 in search of beaver.* [10] Their reports cited many incidents of peaceful contact with Indians.

In 1833, the Joseph Walker expedition documented numerous contacts with Indians while traveling down Mary's River.† However, in one instance, some men in the group caught some Indians

---
* It was on this expedition where the men in the party named the river the Mary's River in honor of Ogden's wife, who was along on this expedition. It was also known as Ogden's River.
† The Mary's River runs west through northern Nevada for approximately 330 miles. The river was renamed for the German naturalist Alexander von Humboldt by explorer John Fremont on his 1844 expedition.

taking the traps set out for beaver, and they took revenge by killing some Indians, at the displeasure of JosephWalker.[11] This event would certainly have fed fear within the Paiute and other tribes living along the Humboldt River*.

John Bidwell, as the scribe for the Bidwell-Bartleson Party of 1841, wrote of their experience:[12] "We saw many Indians on the Humboldt ..." This is the only mention of Indian encounters that Bidwell wrote in the party's journal. It could be assumed that there were no unpleasant encounters between these pioneers and Indians on the way to California.

There were accounts of Indians slipping into emigrant camps at night, shooting arrows into their cattle hoping the animals would die and be left, thus becoming a food source for them. Understandably, this angered the emigrants, but usually no human lives were lost. Adding to the distrust and fear of white men among Indians was one egregious event on August 9, 1845.

Caleb Greenwood, an old mountain man, and his two sons, John and Britton, met up with a group of California-bound emigrants at Fort Hall.† They hired Greenwood to be their guide. Benjamin F. Bonney was an eyewitness and wrote about the event years later:

> *John Greenwood was acting as a pilot one day when an Indian stood up in the sagebrush, frightening*

---

* The Humboldt River was the river followed by hundreds of thousands of emigrants and gold seekers en route to California.
† Fort Hall was a trading post on the Snake River, near present day Pocatello, Idaho.

John A. "Snowshoe" Thompson
Pioneer Mail Carrier of the Sierra

> *John's horse. The horse reared, John jerked hard and the horse nearly threw him. The young man who was riding alongside laughed, and John declared he would kill the Indian. When he aimed his rifle, the Indian threw up his hands; John's companion told him not to shoot, for the Indian meant no harm. The frightened Indian then ran, and young Greenwood shot him through the back. Benjamin's mother laid the dying Indian on a quilt.*[13]

This type of senseless killing would anger any group of people, compelling them to take up arms in defense and revenge.

As time went on, more and more people traveled the Humboldt route. As pioneers built farms and ranches along the Carson River, settling towns such as Dayton, Carson City, Genoa, and Honey Lake, Indians were slowly being displaced. Numerous uncomfortable encounters happened between whites and Indians as land surveying for the Pony Express, the transcontinental telegraph, and the railroad began. Peace treaties were made and broken as some whites and some Indians did not follow or understand the terms of these so-called treaties.

Altogether, these actions changed the Indian way of life in the area forever, continuing to add more instability between the two groups. The final straw, which was credited for the start of Pyramid Lake War, happened in May of 1860 when the Pony Express relay stations were established and mail runs commenced. Important to this war account are Buckland Relay Express Station and Williams' grogshop and trading post, and at times, an express relay station.

Buckland Station was located on the south side of the Carson River about nine miles south of the modern day town of Silver Springs, Nevada, which is on U.S. 50. Williams Station was located about nine or ten miles east of Buckland's on the Carson River.

In May of 1860, news that two young Indian girls were missing spread throughout the Paiute encampment at Pyramid Lake.* Their parents searched for them, following a trail leading to traders named Williams. When the parents talked to the Williams brothers, they claimed they had not seen the girls.[14]

The following day, a Paiute hunter on his way home to Pyramid Lake stopped at Williams Station. The whites at the station wanted to trade with the Indian for his pony, offering a gun, caps, powder, and some lead. The Indian agreed. The trade did not go well as the whites changed their trade agreement and did not want to include the lead. Therefore, the Indian said the trade was not what they had promised and set off to the barn to retrieve his pony. The whites set their dog after the Indian and the Indian was bitten

---

* Pyramid Lake is about thirty miles north of Williams Station.

John A. "Snowshoe" Thompson
Pioneer Mail Carrier of the Sierra

in the leg. Yelling in pain, the Indian kicked the dog away and grabbed his pony.

As he was making his hasty exit, he heard the voices of the two Indian girls rising from beneath the barn floor. Riding swiftly to the Pyramid Lake encampment, he reported hearing the girl's voices to the search party.[15] Soon a raiding party of nine warriors assembled and set out for Williams Station. They staked their ponies near the river and approached the station on foot.

It was May 7, 1860, when four whites stepped outside the station and the Indians confronted them. The surprised and frightened whites denied knowing anything about the girls. One man tried to run away, but was caught and dragged back. The whites tried to defend themselves, but were killed. After the killings, the Indians went to the barn, found the trap door to the cellar and the girls, bound and shaken, but alive.

Only a few whites from Williams Station had kidnapped and sexually assaulted those two Indian girls,[16] but some Indians, wanting revenge, killed all four men at Williams Station*. The Indians proceeded to set fire to the station, burning it to the ground.[17]

A Pony Express rider came through that same day. Finding the station burned and the men dead, he carried the news to Buckland Station. In early 1860, Buckland Station[18] was as far east as the telegraph

---

* Joseph De Certo's version has more than four whites killed at the station.

wires extended at the time, so it is assumed the report was sent by telegraph and immediately reached the newspapers.* [19]

News of the event spread among white communities. It was reported that a "massacre" had occurred at Williams Station, most likely by those not knowing the details of the events leading up to the killings and destruction. Whites wanted revenge. This was a perfect example of how many Indian and white conflicts began, ending badly for all. Entire groups of good people suffered the wrath of vengeance for the lies and bad deeds of a few.

Paiutes were making ready for a retribution attack by whites. The council of chiefs, consisting of Paiute, Shoshoni, and Bannock Indians had assembled to talk of war with whites.[20] The Paiute War Chief Numaga was the lone holdout, not supporting war with whites. For many months before the final event, Numaga reasoned it would only bring destruction upon the People.[21]

To make his point, Numaga spread his body upon the earth and began to fast, praying for the Spirit to bring clear thinking to the others and avoid war.[22] After three days of fasting and suffering, Numaga, in great pain, went to speak to the council of chiefs. He was afforded great respect, but in the end, the vote was for war.

* In 1858, an organization called Placerville, Humboldt, and Salt Lake City Telegraph Company was created to string telegraph lines from California to Salt Lake Valley. The project came to a halt at "Fort Churchill." The fort is located 33.5 miles on U.S. 50 from Carson City, Nevada, and 8.5 miles south of U.S. 50. This would have been Buckland Station as Fort Churchill did not exist until after Pyramid Lake War.

John A. "Snowshoe" Thompson
Pioneer Mail Carrier of the Sierra

Even though Numaga disagreed with the decision, he fulfilled his duties as a war chief and led the warriors into battle.[23]

The Paiutes were ready for war—a war that was long in coming in the minds of many Indians. They were well trained, well armed, well disciplined, and they fought on Indian land they knew well.

Four groups of whites from the communities of Virginia City, Silver City, Carson City, and Genoa were formed into a hasty military.[24] By May 10, 1860, the first group of men, under the command of Major Ormsby, set out for the Truckee River and the Paiute encampment at Pyramid Lake. The weather was cold and blustery. Things would not get much better for this ill-equipped, poorly trained, under-supplied group of men.

Of interest to our study, of course, is John Snowshoe Thompson, who joined the Genoa Rangers under the leadership of Captain Thomas F. Condon, Jr.[25] On May 12, 1860, Thompson's group joined the first group with Major Ormsby.[26] The four groups of angry men fell under the loose leadership of Major William Ormsby from the Carson City Rangers,[27] headquartered at the Big Bend of the Carson River. They reached the Truckee River to search for Indians.

Under the skillful leadership of Chief Numaga, Ormsby was lured into a trap. Numaga had positioned his warriors on both sides of the trail over the ridge leading to Pyramid Lake and the Indian encampment, but out of sight of Ormsby and his men. Numaga had the advantages of numbers, surprise, and the freshness of men and animals. Major Ormsby's men and horses were tired from their long journey. The men had lost their enthusiasm for battle. However, it was too late. Ormsby's one hundred and five men unknowingly rode directly into the deadly ambush.

Indian scouts allowed themselves to be seen by the military groups to lure them into the Indian trap. At just the right moment, the rest of Indian war party—greatly outnumbering the military—made themselves visible. At first Ormsby ordered an attack, but soon realized the error in this command.[28]

"Fall back and regroup" was the next command. However, the terrified and untrained volunteers did not understand the order. In their panic, they dashed for their lives. Indians enclosed the retreating group, with the disastrous results. Seventy-six of the one hundred and five volunteers were killed. Ormsby was one of the first to die.

De Quille related Thompson's near death escape this way:

> Snow-shoe Thompson was out in the war which the people of Nevada* had with the Paiutes, in May 1860, and was in the battle fought at Pyramid Lake, May 12, when the whites were routed with great slaughter. Of the one hundred and five men who went into the fight, seventy-six were killed, and several wounded. Thompson was in the thick of the fight. He was near Major Ormsby, of Carson City, when he fell... His own horse was shot from

---

* It was not yet a state or territory, but was still part of the Utah Territory

John A. "Snowshoe" Thompson
Pioneer Mail Carrier of the Sierra

under him, and for a time he was face to face with several Indians.

When the retreat began, which was general and most disastrous, he struck out on foot for the Truckee River. In speaking of this race for his life, Thompson said: "I pledge you my word, that more than once I wished that the valley was buried in snow, and I was mounted on my snow-shoes."

As he ran for the river, a horse ran after him. The frightened animal kept close to his back, as if seeking his protection. A man cried out to him: "Why don't you get on the horse, which is following behind you?" At this Thompson wheeled about, and as he did so his elbow struck against the animal's nose. It was a horse all saddled and bridled whose owner had fallen in the fight. So Thompson mounted and thus got away. He always said that he believed that the Lord sent him that horse. But for the horse, he would doubtless have been slain....[*] [29]

Hamlin states Snowshoe Thompson was one of the few lucky survivors of this forlorn hope of 1860 and came straggling into Genoa with some friends.[30]

---

[*] For two similar, but differing details of the Paiute War and its eventual outcome, compare the Di Certo version to the Egan version.

"SNOWSHOE" THE MAN

After the fighting subsided, Thompson was with a group of men who helped bring Ormsby's body in to be buried with the others.[31]

When mining activities escalated east of Carson Valley, Snowshoe's mail delivery no longer ended at Genoa. He delivered mail to such mining camps as Gold Canyon, Chinatown (Dayton), Johnstown, and Six-Mile Canyon, and Virginia City as it would soon be established at the head of this canyon.[32]

Thompson met many miners in his travels, but none of such importance as Peter O'Reilley and Pat McLaughlin. While mining their gold claim, they dug up some heavy blue material containing gold.

The gold was good, but they had an inkling the heavy blue material must contain some other type of metal. In June of 1859, they gave Thompson a sample of it, wrapped in a piece of shirting, to be carried to Placerville for analysis.[33]

He took the sample to Professor W. Frank Stewart, the well-known geologist and mining expert, who declared this blue material it to be "silver ore of the richest kind." Stewart's findings were substantiated by assays conducted in Sacramento and Nevada City.[34] Thompson's effort in carrying this sample for assay was to begin the 1859 silver rush, later referred to as the Comstock Lode. It is not clear if Thompson was paid for his delivery of the "blue material" to California, but one would assume he received some type of compensation for that unique request.

He was asked to carry other items over the mountains, but none more unusual than the request

John A. "Snowshoe" Thompson
Pioneer Mail Carrier of the Sierra

by Mrs. L. S. (Eilley) Bowers.* Mrs. Bowers was better known as the "Washoe Seeress" due to her many predictions. Among other things, in the mining community, she was credited with predicting the Comstock discovery.[35] In 1858, Mrs. Bowers kept a boarding house in Johntown,† and she requested Thompson purchase her a "peep-stone" when he next traveled to California.

> *"What is a "peep-stone?" asked Thompson.*
>
> *"It is a ball of glass shaped like an egg," said Mrs. Bowers, "and to be a good one, it should be perfectly transparent. I have one, but it is old and has become cloudy. I want you to find me one that is perfectly clear."*
>
> *"What use do you make of it? What is it good for?" asked Thompson.*
>
> *"I can find out all manner of things with it," said the seeress. "If anything is stolen I can find the thief, and the article stolen. By looking into the peep-stone I can see the faces of the dead; I can trace persons that are missing; I can see hidden treasure, and see rich ore lying deep in the ground.*

---

* Mrs. Bowers was the wife of Lemuel Sanford "Sandy" Bowers who made a fortune in mining and built the Bowers Mansion, ten miles north of Carson City, Nevada. Bowers Mansion Hot Spring is now a Nevada county park.
† Johntown was a small mining camp between Dayton and Gold Hill in Gold Canyon, Nevada.

"Snowshoe" the Man

> *What I now want is a good peep-stone for is to find a mine that I had seen through my old one. It is the richest mine in the world. It is at no great distance from here, but I can't exactly see its surroundings."*[36]

Thompson told Mrs. Bowers that he would try. And try he did. He tried visiting all manner of stores and shops in Sacramento. Most of the time the proprietors had never heard of a peep-stone and, if they had, they did not know where one could be purchased. When Thompson explained how a peep-stone was used, often the proprietors would burst into laughter, with Thompson laughing right along with them. He was never able to find a peep-stone for Mrs. Bowers.[37]

Another instance of Thompson's civic activity and sense of adventure was his part in exploring Lake Tahoe. In 1856, little was known about Lake Tahoe with regards to its actual size, where the lake outlet was located, or the direction in which it flowed.

Thompson, with Asa Hawley and James Green, circumnavigated Lake Tahoe in a rowboat. Hawley described the adventure:

> *In 1856 or 7 it was an open question as to whether there was an outlet to Lake Tahoe or not. Myself, James Green and Snowshoe Thompson made up a party and rowed around the lake in a small boat made by myself. I*

John A. "Snowshoe" Thompson
Pioneer Mail Carrier of the Sierra

put Green in the boat he kept close to the shore and rowed while I paced a half mile to see how fast we traveled, with the wind to ascertaining how long it would take us to navigate the Lake, according to my calculations the lake was 150 miles around it. As we passed around the lake it was plain to us that it had been 2 to 4 feet higher then it was thru this we judge from its washing of the water on the rocks, we found the outlet but at this time we did not know its name but since then it has become known as the Truckee River. I was therefore one of the first men who ever navigated Lake Tahoe and one with Green and Thompson who found the outlet. Since then this lake has become very famous.[38]

7

Other Endeavors

In the latter part of the 1850s, John Thompson was engaged with other activities beyond winter mail delivery over the Sierra.

> *Sacramento Union,* Placerville
> April 28, [1858] 8 p.m.
>
> *Thompson arrived this afternoon, with the express and mail from Carson valley. He brings important news in reference to the new gold digging. The party which left some weeks since to prospect, had returned to Genoa, having found gold fields upon the south fork of Walker's river that prospected 10 to 20 cents to each pan of dirt. The same company had gone back, taking their*

John A. "Snowshoe" Thompson
Pioneer Mail Carrier of the Sierra

families and furniture with them. Thompson says one-third of the people in Carson valley had left, or were making their arrangements to go. The new discoveries cover a large tract of country. Thompson remarks that Major Ormsby will vouch for the truth of the statement, he being now on his way over, bringing what gold the prospecting party obtained. There is no other news of importance.

A dispatch to the *Sacramento Union, May 31,* [1858]:

We have had a call from J. A. Thompson, the Expressman, who has lately arrived from Carson valley. He informs us that there is no snow on the Placerville route, while the Big Tree route, when he was there on Monday last, in a vain attempt to extricate his threshing machine, which he left last fall, there were twelve miles of snow, three feet deep.

He met Dowd, the Expressman, *on that route who had very hard work to get along. We are informed by the arrival of Mr. Hanna, (who came through from Genoa to Old Gulch in*

---

* Augustus T. Dowd appears to have carried the mail on the Big Tree route before Thompson. The Big Tree route went through that grove of redwood trees and around the "biggest" tree in the grove. It is not known if he did this under contract. Appendix J.

eighteen hours) that there is now snow on the route. That threshing machine will be the snow genius for the Union for many a day to come.*¹

It is not clear what Thompson was doing with the threshing machine, or when or where he used it, but it seemed to be of great interest to some. There was a disclaimer article of the previous article, published in Saturday, June 19, 1858, issue of the *San Andreas Independent*. Mr. Hanna contradicted Mr. Thompson on the twelve miles of snow. Perhaps there was some rivalry or jealousy between these two men.

I see by the Sacramento Union, *that Mr. Thompson went up to the threshing machine, and found twelve miles of snow—(twelve miles wide or twelve miles deep?)—on the Big Tree road; met Mr. Dowd on the road who had hard work to get along. Expressman Thompson; as, at first, there was not twelve miles of snow, at that time, on the road—there being snow from one mile north of the summit, to the lower end of Clover Valley, distance of five miles—and from Stanislaus Meadows, to about four hundred yards over the ridge between the Stanislaus and the Mokelumne rivers, a distance of two miles, and with the expectation of about*

---

* The assumption is that this "Union" refers to the *Sacramento Union*

John A. "Snowshoe" Thompson
Pioneer Mail Carrier of the Sierra

four hundred yards, down the slope for Pacific to Mokelumne Valley(s) the road between two points—a distance of seven miles was bars.

Secondly; Expressman, Mr. Thompson, did not meet Expressman Dowd, on the Big Tree road, but at Carson Canyon, three miles from the head of the valley. Mr. Dowd says he is thinking Mr. Thompson would have harder work hauling his machine over the Hangtown road, if he tried, than he had riding through to Carson Valley.

If Thompson has wanted to take his machine over to Placerville, it is likely he would have done so, as he says there was less than a mile of snow on the west side of the Sierra Nevada, at the pass, and downhill at that. Mr. V. Shearer went over the Big Tree route last year, with a wagon and 3,500 lbs. of freight, when there was more snow on the summit than at the time Mr. Thompson speaks of: only in the morning when the snow has froze hard. The "Masheen" is surely the now-myth of the Union.[2]

It would appear that Thompson had a lucrative business of not only hauling freight over the mountains, but also of transporting people, by keeping the trails open in the winter for "wagon travel." Most

Other Endeavors

of what is written of these businesses is taken from newspaper accounts.

>Placerville, Dec. 10, 1858
>
>*In to-day's* Union *allusion is made to the failure of the Central Mail contractors to consummate their agreement with Thompson to keep the route open over the summit. The* Union *is correct in its statement. But from documents shown to me by one of the contractors, I am satisfied that the failure, in this instance, was unavoidable. Thomson has just arrived from Carson Valley, and informs me that the matters have been so arranged that he can immediately commence operation and he will lose no time in getting ready for his Winter's task.*[3]
>
>Placerville, Dec.18, 1858
>
>*Thompson, the expressman, and Mark Smith started for Lake Valley today, with two wagons heavily laden with goods for Lake and Carson Valleys. This freight will be hauled about 80 miles on Thompson's sleighs. Those who have crossed the Summit since the snow plows were brought into requisition are in ecstasies about the excellence of the road. All agree that the jaunt is more of*

John A. "Snowshoe" Thompson
Pioneer Mail Carrier of the Sierra

a pleasure trip than otherwise. In fact, a party of ladies and gentlemen at Genoa have made arrangements to take a sleigh ride over the mountains, and spend the holidays among us.[4]

Carson Valley-New Road, etc.

By the arrival of a friend from Carson Valley, who was formerly a resident of this city, we learn that the road over the mountains, so far from being obstructed by snow, is really much better than in summer. The snow has covered the rocks and rough ground, and the sleigh runs above them on the packed snow.

Thompson has two sleighs and two teams of mules with which he travels the road daily. His headquarters are in Lake Valley,* and his plan is to start one team west and the other east. That traveling west comes over the summit and as far as Silver Creek, where it strikes the new road down the American River. To that point wagons manage to haul goods, and there Thompson takes them on his sleigh and runs them over to Lake Valley.

The next morning the team for the mouth of Carson Cañon is harnessed to the sleigh, upon which the goods are loaded; the other starts back to Silver

---
* South Lake Tahoe

OTHER ENDEAVORS

Creek* for another load. The sleigh for the mouth of the Carson Cañon delivers its freight at Woodford's which is twelve miles from Lake Valley, and from there it is hauled to Genoa, eleven miles further, in a wagon. It is about thirteen miles from Lake Valley to Silver creek, which makes the distance traveled on snow twenty-five miles. The sub-Indian Agent for the Indians on the east side of the Sierra Nevada, Frederick Dodge, who came over from Carson in the stage day before yesterday, declares that portion traveled in sleighs to be really a pleasure trip.[5]

In 1859, Thompson claimed 160 acres in Diamond Valley under the Preemption Act of 1841. This act allowed squatters—who were heads of households, widows, or single men over twenty-one on government land—and who were citizens of the United States, or intended to become naturalized, and who lived on the land for fourteen months to purchase up to 160 acres at a very low price (not less than $1.25 per acre) before the land was offered for sale to the public.[6]

To qualify for this land ownership, Thompson applied for citizenship. His application was written in the formal clerk's handwriting of 1866, and is difficult to decipher.

In District Court 16th Jud. Dist. County of Alpine and State of

---
* Silver Fork, near Kyburz on U.S. 50.

John A. "Snowshoe" Thompson
Pioneer Mail Carrier of the Sierra

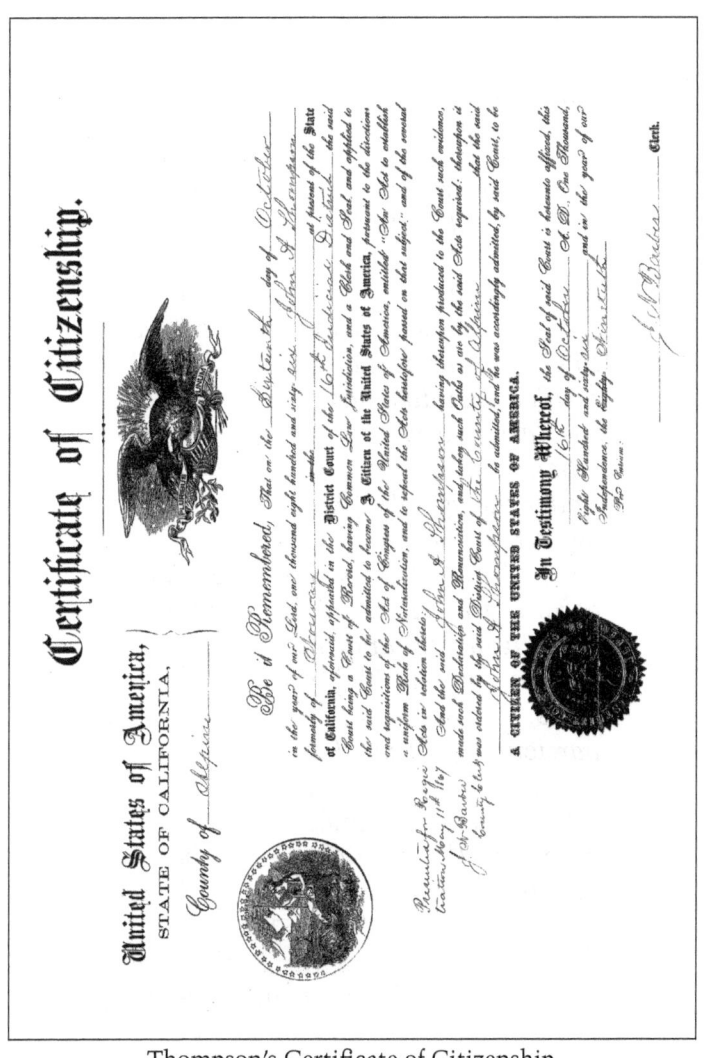

Thompson's Certificate of Citizenship
Courtesy: Alpine County Museum

OTHER ENDEAVORS

California Application of John A. Thompson to become a citizen of the United States.

John A. Thompson being duly sworn says that he was born in the Kingdom of Norway, and came to the United States in the year 1837 and landed in New York, that he has resided continuously in the United States since said time, that he came to California in the year 1851 and has resided therein since said time and for the last five years continuously, that when he came to New York he was under the age of eighteen to wit, of the age ten years.

That it was his intention in coming to United States to renounce all allegiance and fidelity to every foreign [unreadable] *power potentate state or sovereignty what ever and particularly the King of Norway whose subject he is, and it is now his intention to renounce and become a citizen of the United States,wherefore he, Subscribed and sworn to before me this 16*[th] *day of October 1866*
Jin. Barber, Clerk
John A. Thompson [signed][7]

After claiming his 160 acres in Diamond Valley, Thompson set out to build a small cabin , where he lived for the remainder of his life. He

John A. "Snowshoe" Thompson
Pioneer Mail Carrier of the Sierra

Thompson's Cabin *Courtesy: Alpine County Museum*

Thompson-made Rocking Chair
Courtesy: Douglas County Historical Society

OTHER ENDEAVORS

developed his land and farm and seemed to make a go of it. Following is an account from the Carson Valley Historical Society (CVHS) publication of just one major undertaking:

> *Thompson learned how to construct irrigation ditches from "Lucky Bill" Thorrington who lived in Genoa.***[8] *Thompson built two ditches to take water to his Diamond Valley ranch from the West Fork of the Carson River. At the time, ditches seemed quite a phenomena to the other ranchers because it looked like they were carrying the water uphill. Known as Thompson's Ditch No. 1 and Thompson's Ditch No. 2, they are still in use today."*†[9]

By comparing the property tax records, it seems that Thompson's possessions increased over time.

Assessment Rolls Alpine Co. 1865
J. A. Thompson
Township 4 Value $1500

The right of possession in and to one ranch of 160 acres, more or less,

---

* "Next to Knott, he (Thorrington) was the most enterprising and progressive man in the Nevada Territory during the 1850s." (Note: Nevada did not become a territory until 1861.)
† Thompson's two ditches can still be seen on modern maps.

John A. "Snowshoe" Thompson
Pioneer Mail Carrier of the Sierra

situated in the lower end of Diamond Valley and joined on the west by E. W. Trimmer's Ranch and on the east by unoccupied land with a house and other improvements.

1 wagon $25, 2 cows, 2 calves $50, 5 horses, 1 hog $150, Farming $25. State tax $25.88 County tax $36.00, Hospital Tax $1.12, School Tax $4.50, road Tax $1.13, Court House/Jail Tax $10.12 total $78.73.[10]

In 1851, Thompson contracted "gold fever" and came to California to seek his fortune. It seems he was similarly afflicted in 1867 as the records show Thompson became involved with mining at Silver Mountain.*

Assessment Rolls 1867
J. A. Thompson
The right of possession in lots 1, 7 & 8 in Block 20 in Town of Silver Mountain. Value: $250, State Tax $2.83, County, $4.00, school $.62, Court House/Jail $.80 Other, $.50. Total $8.25.

The assessment book entry for 1869 is a bit curious, because it is not clear whether this refers to Silver Mountain or Diamond Valley. Perhaps it was

---
* Silver Mountain was a thriving mining town, originally called Konigsberg. See Appendix K.

OTHER ENDEAVORS

Diamond Valley, as noted by the higher value of his wagon. However, it listed cows, horses, and included furniture. Another curious note is the value was lower compared to the tax bill recorded in 1865.

Assessment Book Value 1869
J. A. Thompson
1 wagon $50, 8 cows 7 calves, $4.65.
5 Horses 1 hog, $2.65, furniture $50.
Farming implements $30
Total Value $860
Total Tax: $28.92[11]

In 1871, Thompson harvested 1,600 bushels of oats and barley and more hay than any other farmer in the county.[12] His lands had increased in size as well as all his holdings and value. Note, too, that horses and hogs were valued separately in that tax year.

Assessment Rolls 1871
J. A. Thompson

The right of possession in and to a tract of land in Diamond Valley and known as Thompson Ranch, also 1/4 interest (undivided) in a ditch commencing at Wades Mill near Woodfords and running there to Thompson Ranch.
2 wagons, $100, farming implements $250, 19 horses $500, 12 cows $480,
10 calves $100, 8 stock cattle $160,
Hogs $40. Furniture $50. Chicks $40.

John A. "Snowshoe" Thompson
Pioneer Mail Carrier of the Sierra

Number of acres 200, value $2000.
Value of improvements $500.
Taxes paid $147.58 November 1, 1871[13]

From these tax rolls it can be seen that Thompson kept busy with his farming, mining, freighting supplies and people, mail delivery in the winter, and working to plow snow to keep the trail open for wagons, as will be detailed shortly. Thompson offered his land for pasturage to other people for their animals for $1.50 per month at his Diamond Valley ranch.*[14]

A major event in the life of John Thompson was his marriage to Agnes Singleton, who was best described in the CVHS publication:

> *In May 1866 Thompson married a gracious and charming English woman named Agnes Singleton. She was born on Nov. 4, 1831, in Preston, Lancashire, England to Thomas Singleton and Ann Hall. Agnes came to America in 1864 with her stepmother Anne Beech Singleton to visit Agnes' brother Samuel in Carson Valley.*
>
> *Anne and Agnes decided they wanted to remain in America and accepted a job keeping house for John*

---

* This advertisement was found to run weekly in March and April, 1873.

Other Endeavors

"Snowshoe" Thompson at his home in Diamond Valley in 1864. Two years later John and Agnes were married at Samuel Singleton's home in Sheridan.[*] [15]

Portrait of Arthur Thompson
Courtesy: Douglas County Historical Society

---

* Sheridan town is south of the new Kingsbury Grade monument on NV SR 206-Foothill Road.

John A. "Snowshoe" Thompson
Pioneer Mail Carrier of the Sierra

This seems like an interesting coincidence, since John's mother, Gro, had been his father's housekeeper before she married his father.* Just before John and Agnes were married, "John added two rooms and an attic to his dugout"† [16] in Diamond Valley.

Arthur's Cradle made by Thompson
Courtesy: Douglas County Historical Society

John's life was about to make another dramatic change nine months after he married Agnes. On February 11, 1867, she gave birth to a baby boy, whom they named Arthur Thomas. The proud father made a cradle out of a sluice box.

John was so excited about his son that he could not wait for him to grow older and go snowshoeing.

---
* See Chapter 1.
† A dugout was a form of pioneer cabin.

OTHER ENDEAVORS

For the child's first Christmas, John made Arthur a tiny pair of snowshoes (skis).[17]

A terrifying incident took place in 1871 while the family wintered in Silver Mountain on John's 1867 mining claim.

Snowshoe decided to spend the winter prospecting at Silver Mountain (formerly Konigsberg) about twenty miles south of Diamond Valley. Silver Mountain was primarily a settlement of Norwegian people. Agnes and Arthur, four years old, moved with him for that winter.

Elma S. Bradshaw, a great niece of Agnes wrote about the Silver Mountain incident:

> *While continuing his regular mail delivery over the Sierras [Sierra] and also farming activities, in addition Snowshoe had been doing a little prospecting on Silver Mountain. One evening he announced his intentions of staying up at the mine that winter and working it in between his mail runs. There was a small, primitive cabin on top of the hill near the mine where he could sleep after his digging, but Agnes protested.*
>
> *She did not like the idea of him staying up there alone during so much of the winter, so she insisted that he take her along. He knew it was*

John A. "Snowshoe" Thompson
Pioneer Mail Carrier of the Sierra

no place for a woman, but she would have her way—knowing that she could "keep the cabin warm for him to come home to and have a hot meal ready for him to enjoy."

Before the snow began to fall, Snowshoe carried to the mine the supplies necessary for their stay there, and Agnes prepared the needful clothes, bedding and personal essentials they would need.

Everything went well for a time while they lived in a small mine cabin, but one evening when Snowshoe was away on a mail trip, little Arthur became very ill...breathing heavily and delirious with high temperature.

Agnes was very much relieved when her husband finally arrived home the following day, for he always seemed to know what to do. Though she had given their sick child what homemade remedies she could devise, she knew they must take him to Genoa, several hours away, where the only doctor was.

"Snowshoe" was a man of action and few words, so as soon as he viewed the situation, he walked to the tool shed that held his mining gear, and began preparing a "contraption" with which to get his wife and child down off the mountain.

Other Endeavors

He cut some straps of leather, made a sling of them, and said to his wife, "Agnes, I'll put my arms through these two loops and fasten the other strap around my waist. If you sit in the sling, put your arms around my neck and your legs around my waist, I know I can get you down off the hill. The baby I will carry in my arms, while you ride on my back."

Agnes gasped, "You are going to carry the two of us down that steep hill! Oh, John, you can't".

"It has got to be done," he said. "There is no other way. While you are wrapping Arthur up, I'll throw your snowshoes down the hill. You can use them after we get down farther."

Arthur was a husky boy of four years, and Agnes thought of her hundred and fifteen pounds, and after she had climbed into the sling her husband had rigged up, she just closed her eyes and held her breath.

After they were safely down the mountain, they still had to go to a mining camp nearby where the men helped them to build a sledge to place Arthur on to get him all the way to Genoa. When they were near enough so that Agnes wouldn't lose her way,

John A. "Snowshoe" Thompson
Pioneer Mail Carrier of the Sierra

> *John hurried ahead of her with Arthur to the doctor's home.*
>
> *He diagnosed Arthur's illness as a mild attack of lung fever [pneumonia], and due to the boy's youth and good health, he soon rallied after a few days.*[18]

In the late 1850s, the demand for mail delivery was growing in other parts of northern California, including Murphys.*

In 1860, the Pony Express was making regular ten-day runs from St. Joseph, Missouri, to Placerville, over the California Trail, which included the route from Genoa to Placerville. In addition, the transcontinental telegraph was soon to be completed.

> *San Andreas Independent*
> *October 8, 1859*
>
> *We expect to hear in a few days that California is to be immediately united to the Atlantic by telegraph, under the direction of Peter Cooper of New York and others....The immediate construction of the work and enterprise have been definitely determined upon;*

---

* The town of Murphys, California, is 8.8 miles southeast on SR 4, off SR 49 near Angels Camp. Snowshoe used the 1856 Big Tree Road, which cut off from Hope Valley and the California Trail's Carson River Route, to where Calaveras Big Trees State Park is now located, then southwest on SR 4 for fifteen miles to Murphys.

OTHER ENDEAVORS

and within a year from this date we expect to dish up to our readers exclusive daily telegraph items from New York – Evening Bulletin.

Thompson's mail delivery route changed to different routes and destinations with the coming of the Pony Express. Mail still needed to be delivered to other locations, including Murphys, by way of the Big Tree Road. This road ran from its southwest end at Murphys, then followed east along modern day CA SR 4 to Hermit Valley, then turned north to its northwest end at Hope Valley, near the junction of CA SR 88 and 89.[19]

The Big Tree Road* was opened to wagon travel in 1856 by a group of investors, whose purpose was to divert the wagon migration from the main Carson River Route in Hope Valley to Murphys and the southern mines of the Mother Lode. This plan to divert traffic realized moderate success until the Comstock Lode hit in 1859.

San Andreas Independent,
Saturday, May 21, 1859

New Mail Routes

The Post Master General contemplates organizing the following new mail and post routes in California:

---

* The use of singular "Tree" referenced the biggest tree that the road went around. The state park is called Calaveras Big Trees State Park, referencing the many big redwood trees in the grove.

John A. "Snowshoe" Thompson
Pioneer Mail Carrier of the Sierra

> *1st. A weekly mail from Murphys in Calaveras County over the Big Tree road to Carson Valley in Utah Territory. 2d. A weekly mail from Rabbit Creek in Sierra county via Quincy in Plumas county, to Susanville, Honey Lake in same territory. 3d. A weekly mail from Bidwell's Bar, via Noble's Pass to Susanville, Honey Lake in same territory. 4th. A weekly mail from Genoa in Carson Valley via Eagle to Washo and Long valley, to Susanville in Honey Lake Valley. 5th. A weekly route from Carson Valley road on the Humboldt. This last will connect at the forks with the overland mail route from St. Paul, Minnesota via South Pass, Salt Lake City to Oregon and California. It enters the latter via Noble's Pass.[20]*

From about 1860 to 1864, Thompson delivered mail to Murphys via Hope Valley by way of the Big Tree Road. In 1860, when silver was discovered in Konigsberg,* later known as Silver Mountain City, California, a more direct route was needed from Murphys to the silver mines at Konigsberg, Monitor, and other mines in the surrounding Markleville area.

Work began immediately on a road that would branch from the Big Tree Road at Hermit Valley and would be a more direct easterly route over the

---

* Konigsberg/Silver Mountain City. See Appendix K

summit, which became known as Ebbetts Pass. The section of the Big Tree Road going north from Hermit Valley to Hope Valley was no longer needed and fell into disuse. Today this is a popular four-wheel drive road for only the most serious drivers.

A newspaper account in the *Weekly Calaveras Chronicle* explained Thompson's mail route, which used some previously quoted material:

> *February 15, 1862*
> Mr. Thompson has carried the mail during the winter from the Big Trees over the mountains to Washoe. He makes the journey over and back, on foot, carrying the mail on his person. The snow on the heights above the trees is several feet in depth....
> Instead of wearing the ordinary snow shoes, the mail carrier uses long wooden skates common in the north of Europe. These skates are five or six feet in length, turning up in the front like a sleigh runner; the foot is fastened to the board by a leather band, with a ridge under the hallow of the boot, which prevents it from slipping back.
> Thus prepared with a strong pole to guide him, he slips along over the snow with astonishing speed; on the down grade he rests himself partially on the pole, and slides down the hill as swiftly as a school boy can on his sled.

John A. "Snowshoe" Thompson
Pioneer Mail Carrier of the Sierra

> *When coming over the brow of the mountains, near one of the stations on the road, he sounds his horn, and here the inmates of the house can fairly get out of the door to meet him, he is there before them, sliding down the acclivity with almost the quickness of thought.*
>
> *Mr. Thompson has not failed, but on one occasion, to make his trip regularly every week; solitary and alone he pursues his journey over the mountains and through valleys, while around him there is nothing but a waste of snow.*
>
> *He is sometimes delayed by the fierce storms of the Sierras [sic], when he obliged to seek shelter under a tree from the falling snow... It requires a stout heart to brave all the dangers of the trip, but California furnishes hardy men, who can endure almost anything but a flooded Capitol.*[*] [21]

Then in 1864, upon completion of the Ebbetts Pass route (CA SR 4), Thompson would follow that more direct route from Genoa to Markleeville, to Silver Mountain City, and into Murphys.

---

[*] Before the levy system was in place in northern California, the Sacramento valley and town would flood several feet each year. Many buildings had second story entrances for use during the flooding.

8

THE BIRTH OF THE SKI SPORT

John Thompson may or may not have been the first to use the Norwegian style "snow skates" in California. The Norwegian snow skates were introduced in 1853 and people began using them to travel from place to place.[1] Snowshoe Thompson was also using snow skates (skis) in 1853 when working for Thomas Knott.[2]

In 1856, at least three years after Thompson delivered mail for Knott, a similar activity was happening 115 miles to the north of Placerville in the small community of La Porte, California, in an area referred to by some as the "Lost Sierra."[3]

La Porte came about by myth and the hope of a great gold discovery of a "lake where the shores were lined with gold."[4] Many of those who came to seek their fortune were Scandinavians, who had disembarked in San Francisco, and found their way to the "Lost Sierra."[5]

La Porte sits on a plateau just south of and

John A. "Snowshoe" Thompson
Pioneer Mail Carrier of the Sierra

above the Feather River. It is south of Quincy, California, on the Quincy-La Porte road, at an elevation of about five thousand feet. Even though it is at a much lower elevation than where Thompson traveled on his mail runs, its more northern latitude provides an abundance of winter snow.

When crossing over the high passes of the Sierra on his various mail runs, Thompson would reach elevations of: 9,600 feet at West Pass; 8,575 feet at Carson Pass; 7,377 feet at Echo Summit; 7,735 feet at Luther Pass; and 7,344 feet at Daggett. On the Big Tree route, Thompson would reach elevations of 8,732 feet at Ebbetts Pass and 8,315 feet at Border Ruffian Pass. These passes were all part of Thompson's regular mail runs. This information is important to put the upcoming events into perspective.

During the harsh long winters in La Porte and adjacent communities, there was a desire—and a need—for the inhabitants to visit or communicate with each other. In addition, during the long winter when mining activities ceased or became difficult because of the deep snow, people switched to using skis for recreation.

The idea was to make very long skis and create a straight downhill course to see who could go the fastest. These long skis were known as "long boards." They were from ten and a half feet to thirteen and a half feet in length, varying in weight between thirteen and seventeen pounds per pair.[6] Men using these long boards could gain speeds up to ninety miles per hour.

These ski racers had developed the invention known as "dope, which was a mixture of various waxes and sap from different trees. This "dope" was

The Birth of the Ski Sport

rubbed on the bottom of the skis to prevent the snow from sticking and to make the long boards run faster. They learned that one dope mixture would work better for one snow condition and another mixture worked better for a different condition.[7]

The skiers of La Porte were not the only ones who enjoyed recreational skiing. At Silver Mountain, where Snowshoe Thompson had a cabin and a mine, the people also played in the snow, as seen from this newspaper article.

> *Silver Mountain Correspondence*
> *Silver Mountain, Alpine County*
> *February 1865*
>
> *Editor* Chronicle: *I write you from this "Eagles' nest" in the mountains, to let your readers know how we spend this wintery weather, and what has transpired among us since winter came.*
>
> *Our Winter is no mockery; it comes according to the almanac and tells us earnestly that it is here. We have in town about two feet of snow, and from four to five on the mountains around us. Our Winter sports are mostly confined to dancing parties and sliding down hill on Norwegian snow-skates. At the former are a goodly number of ladies, of whom we have about eighty, and the latter affords a vast amount of fun for the whole town.*

John A. "Snowshoe" Thompson
Pioneer Mail Carrier of the Sierra

Large numbers climb the sides of the mountain in sight of town, almost daily, for the purpose of sliding down, and it is truly wonderful to see with what speed and precision they can descend.

The Norwegians of course take the lead, for they have been accustomed to the use of this kind of snow skate from childhood. That those who have never seen a pair of snow skates may understand something of them, I will give a description of how they are constructed.

They consist each of a strip of tough wood about twelve feet long, by from four to five inches in width, and about one and a half inches thick in the center, tapering to about half that thickness at the ends.

The front end is turned up like a sled-runner. In the contre,* *a cleet [sic] or a few thicknesses of leather are nailed across, on which stands the hollow of the foot, and a strap about three inches in width passes over the toe of the boot and is fastened to the sides of the skate.*

The party using them usually carry a stick about eight feet long with which to balance themselves.

---

* French word meaning "against."

THE BIRTH OF THE SKI SPORT

Beginners can go along quite well on the level ground, but when they attempt running down hill it is quite difficult, and requires considerable practice to keep on the feet.

When one loses his balance, he is plunged into the snow, perhaps entirely out of sight, and is greeted with a laugh from the lookers on. His skates sometimes go on swiftly down the hill and he is left in a helpless condition, until someone takes them back to him... Among our best performers on these skates, is the express man, Thompson, who carried the mails and express all winter, from Genoa, in Carson Valley to Murphys, in Calaveras County, on skates.

He, with several others, a few days since, came down the mountain east of town, about a quarter of a mile, where the descent was at least forty-five degrees, and runs through a row of posts, set for a fence, at the bottom.

They performed the trip without falling. To call such traveling, railroad speed is but a tame comparison. Mr. Thompson has a valuable ranch in what is called Diamond Valley, three miles east of Woodford's at the mouth of Carson Cañon, which he tills.[8]

John A. "Snowshoe" Thompson
Pioneer Mail Carrier of the Sierra

Background information as to how Snowshoe Thompson raced with the La Porte boys is presented in the following articles.

Mountain Messenger,*⁹
March 6, 1869

We have often heard of the famous Snow-Shoe runner by the name of Thompson, but never knew until recently that he was a tangible, a living reality. Mr. Thompson had heard of snowshoe races, and to satisfy his curiosity he attended those recently held at La Porte. He veni vidied *but did not* vici *a bit.*† *In fact when he saw some of our runners make a trip he said he did not want any in his.*

There is no doubt but that Thompson is a good traveler on the snow, but he had the frankness to acknowledge when he saw the boys run, that he knew nothing about racing. The shoes brought along by Thompson were a curiosity.

It is reported that they were turned up at both ends, about seven

---
* The *Mountain Messenger* was a newspaper published in Downieville, California.
† Could it be a play on Julius Caesar's words when he described how/what he did on his campaign? veni (I came), vidi (I saw), vici (I conquered), but meaning Snowshoe came, saw, but did not conquer?

THE BIRTH OF THE SKI SPORT

feet long, convex on the bottom, and innocent of any acquaintance with "dope." In fact he never knew what dope was until he saw it at the races. The Union gave notice that Mr. Thompson was coming up to put our boys on this metal. Will it now state that Thompson was an extensive failure as a racer?[10]

The following article appeared in the *Alpine Chronicle* as Thompson's response to the *Mountain Messenger* article. It appears that he was not pleased with their reporting.

SNOW-SHOE CHALLENGE:

The following challenge is offered on behalf of Snow Shoe Thompson and the Alpine boys.

Editors: **Alpine Chronicle**:
The Downieville Messenger says I had heard of snow shoe races, and to satisfy my curiosity, I attended those at La Porte, expecting to see some scientific snow shoe racing, but I was disappointed; it was nothing but "dope racing" and is unworthy of the name of snow shoeing. It is nothing more than a little improvement on coasting down the hill on a handsled.
The improvement is that

John A. "Snowshoe" Thompson
Pioneer Mail Carrier of the Sierra

instead of uprights and crossbars from one runner to the other they make their legs and crouch answer this purpose, and they no more have control over their shoes than a boy has over his sled. They exhibited some skill in making dope, but all they gain in this is that they make about the same time on a hill of 15 degrees that a man without dope on a hill of 30 degrees.

The "dope riders" at La Porte are good clever fellows, but they have no more right to call themselves scientific snow shoers than a man with steel skates on smooth ice, who with a spiked pole placed between his legs, pushes himself straight ahead, should be called a scientific skater.

Now, I, on behalf of the Alpine Boys, make these propositions to the Plumas and Sierra Boys or "any other man" in the state: come to Alpine county next winter and run with us. We will run you for $1,000 a side for each one of the following, viz:

First: Against time: you select your hillside, and then we will select ours.

Second: Side-by-side; we to select the hillside.

Third: Over a precipice fifteen-feet high, without the use of a pole, the one jumping the furtherest without falling to take the purse.

The Birth of the Ski Sport

Fourth: *From the top to the bottom of the highest and heaviest -timbered mountain we can find.*

Fifth: *and last run to be from the top of Silver Mountain Peak to the town of Silver Mountain the altitude of the Peak is 11,000 feet, 4,000 feet above town, and a distance four miles.*

Now, boys of Plumas and Sierra, come over here; we will treat you well, and if you win our money you are welcome. If you come, be sure and bring that **Messenger** *man along with you, and I will bet him $100 that if he attempts to follow me on snow shoes for one day he will break his neck before night. For the information of those who have not seen my snow shoes I will give the dimensions: They are 9 feet long; turned up in front and flat-bottomed; 4 inches wide in front, 3½ inches behind, and 1½ inches thick in the center.*

 J. A. Thompson
(Snowshoe Thompson)

The *Alpine Chronicle* added the following comment to Thompson's challenge:

As the **Messenger** *rather disparaged our man we will cite what he has done, and can do it again for an object: Mr. Thompson with a heavy*

John A. "Snowshoe" Thompson
Pioneer Mail Carrier of the Sierra

bag upon his back has frequently run for three miles in five minutes; he has jumped precipices and landed ninety feet, right side up, from the starting point; he has command of his shoes to such an extent that on the steepest and heaviest-timbered mountains he glides among the obstructions like the skater on ice; at ever so great a speed he will touch or pass within a inch of any designated object; he has often carried the mail from Genoa to Placerville eighty miles in fifteen hours running time; he runs standing, and in coming down the mountain he does not check himself with the pole, but turns when he wants to stop. Now, we have stated what one of the Alpine boys has done, and can do. We hope this challenge will be accepted. We accept the wager of the hundred dollars against our Messenger friend's neck.
—Alpine Chronicle[11]

The La Porte boys never took up the challenge. As early as 1860 informal ski clubs were formed to fill the long winter months to have fun and challenge others to slide downhill as fast as one could. The first formally organized "snowshoe" or ski club was the "Alturas Snowshoes Club," formed in La Porte in December of 1866. The first documented competition

THE BIRTH OF THE SKI SPORT

in the United States was held the following February on Lexington Hill in La Porte.[12]

Soon neighboring communities created their own racetracks that ranged from eight hundred to eighteen hundred feet long. The competitive sport of long board skiing was born.[13] The Alturas Snowshoes Club was the first club in the world to organize for the specific purpose of snowshoe competition.[14]

Along with it came a multi-billion dollar skiing industry. Currently there are ten or more ski resorts in the greater Lake Tahoe basin—Snowshoe Thompson's environs. There are tens of thousands, if not hundreds of thousands, of people who enjoy downhill and cross country skiing, along with devotees to modern day snowshoeing.

The following article, printed in the *Mountain Democrat* in Placerville, California, on April 13, 1889, further illustrated how quickly the sport of ski completion grew in popularity and just how significant was the contribution of John A. Thompson. This is a wonderful article, and even though there might be a bit of exaggeration and inaccuracy, it shows the love and respect for Thompson.

JUMPING DOWN A MOUNTAIN
Snowshoe Thompson's
Remarkable leap of 180 feet

The sport of "ski" or snowshoe running, so long popular in the Sierra Nevada Mountains [sic] *is beginning to be*

John A. "Snowshoe" Thompson
Pioneer Mail Carrier of the Sierra

practiced in some of the northern... Atlantic states. An eastern exchange says: "Ski running, a Scandinavian sport, is becoming popular in Minnesota. The performer slides down hill on long wooden skates, or foot toboggans, and at a prepared jolt makes a leap into space. Ninety-five feet is the longest ski jump on record in Norway.

Ninety-five feet seems a immense leap, but it has been so far surpassed in the Sierras [Sierra] *that no easterner need ever try for the championship. The champion ski runner and leaper of the world is John A. Thompson—better known as "Snowshoe Thompson"—who died in Alpine county, Cal, about thirteen years ago.**

Thompson was born at Upper Tins [sic]*, Prestijeld* [sic]*, Norway, April 30, 1827, and died at his home in the Sierras* [Sierra] *May 15, 1876. He was the father of snowshoe runners of the mountain counties of California. He made the first pair of Norwegian snowshoes ever seen on the Pacific coast.*

Thompson's greatest leap was made on the side of a steep mountain just west of the town of Genoa, Douglas

---

* John Snowshoe Thompson's death is discussed in Chapter 10.

The Birth of the Ski Sport

county. Darting down the side of the steep mountain he made a leap of 180 feet. This leap is vouched for by W. P. Merrill, postmaster at Woodfords in the high Sierras [Sierra], and by several citizens of Genoa. The leap was made from a terrace half way down the side of the mountain, and the leaper landed in a drift of snow over fifty feet in depth, where for a time he was buried out of sight.

C. B. Gregory (now deceased), who was for some years neighbor to Snowshoe Thompson in the mountains, said in speaking of the feat of the great leaper: "I did not see him make his great jump off the side of the mountain back in Genoa, but I have often seen him make leaps of fifty and sixty feet at Silver Mountain, Alpine county.

The people of Silver Mountain mining camp were want to amuse themselves by descending a big mountain near town and then darting down to the valley below on their snowshoes. They had a starting point about half way up the side of the mountain. Snowshoe Thompson sometimes joined these parties of ski runners. He was not satisfied with a run down half a mountain, he wanted it all. He would circle round till he had reached the highest peak of the

John A. "Snowshoe" Thompson
Pioneer Mail Carrier of the Sierra

big mountain. He would then utter the wild war cry of the old Northmen and then with his balance pole poised horizontally before him in both hands, would come flying down the side of the mountain like a fiend of the wind. When he came near to the crowd of towns people standing midway down the mountain, Thompson would stoop almost to the ground then suddenly springing up would go sailing through the air high above the men and women watching the descent.

At times he would make several leaps each of from fifty to eighty feet in a single descent. His leaping was not a little like "sky flying."

Snowshoe Thompson was a very sinewy and powerful man. He stood six feet in his stockings and weighed 180 pounds. He had blond hair and beard and the blue eyes of his Scandinavian ancestors, the old sea roving Northmen...Virginia City Enterprise[15]

THE BIRTH OF THE SKI SPORT

Map of Chorpenning's Western Mail Delivery Routes
Courtesy: Alpine County Museum

John A. "Snowshoe" Thompson
Pioneer Mail Carrier of the Sierra

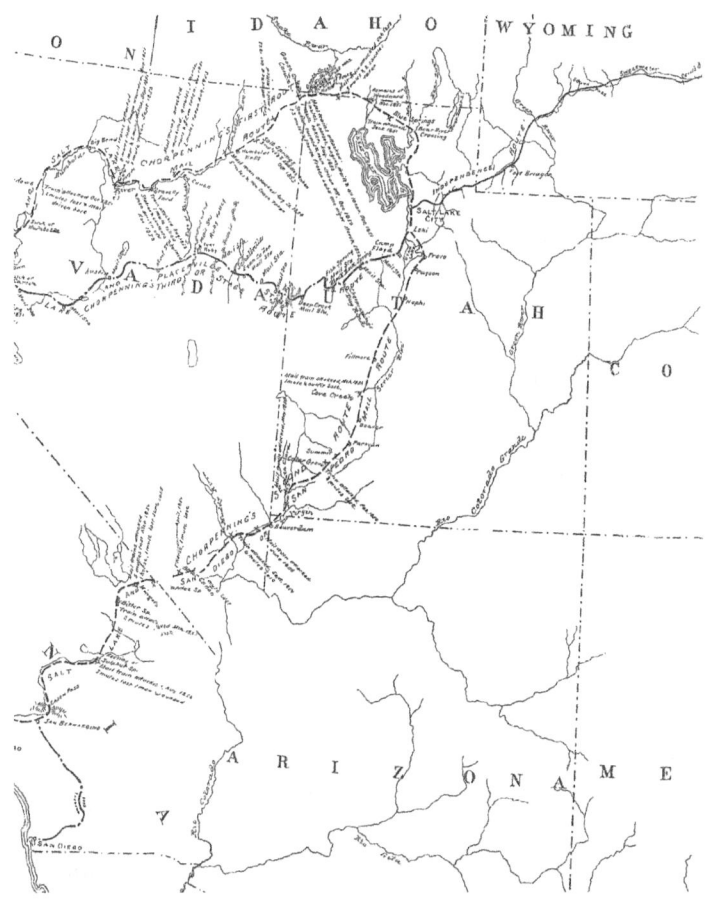

Map of Chorpenning's Eastern Mail Delivery Routes
Courtesy: Alpine County Museum

9

Snowshoe Thompson Was Never Paid...or Was He?

When reading about Snowshoe, that gnawing question keeps returning—why did the Post Office Department never pay him?

The research on this subject is most interesting and rather convoluted with what appears to be many inconsistencies—one might dare say downright lying by some postal officials and mismanagement by mail delivery contractors.

These contracts were authorized by congress and issued by the Postmaster General. As noted in Chapter 4, Absalom Woodward and George Chorpenning received the first mail delivery contract between Salt Lake City, Utah Territory, and Sacramento, California, April 25, 1851.* The contract was for Postal Route No. 5066, for the sum of $14,000 per year.

---

* The Second Assistant Postmaster General to United States Court of Claims regarding George Chorpenning's claim.

John A. "Snowshoe" Thompson
Pioneer Mail Carrier of the Sierra

Chorpenning experienced financial difficulties from the very start, and it appeared that he and the postmaster general were at odds with each other. It began when Chorpenning's first contract was annulled by the postmaster general on November 19, 1852, and issued to another person, W. L. Blanchard for $50,000.[1]

As stated earlier, Chorpenning set out for Washington, D.C., to plead his case to a new postmaster general. The contract was reinstated, with his amount adjusted to $30,000 and he was given permission to alter his route via San Pedro, California, during the winter.[2]

Chorpenning filed several petitions over the years to the United States Court of Claims and the United States Supreme Court for his financial losses and requests for his contracts to be reinstated. He was somewhat successful with the courts, but the conflicts would continue. The new postmaster general annulled the next two contracts, which Chorpenning challenged repeatedly in court. He would be in and out of court until 1876, when he lost his final case.

Here begins an attempt to sort out the complex issue regarding Thompson's payment, or non-payment, for his dedication to delivering the mail for twenty years. Who hired him and who should have paid Thompson is even more confusing.

Since contracts were issued to mail contractors by the postmaster general to deliver the mail between California and Utah Territory, it seems logical that the contractors would hire and pay Thompson and others who helped to deliver the mail. Yet, research shows

Snowshoe Thompson Was Never Paid...
Or Was He?

that Thompson interacted with the postmasters in Placerville and Genoa for his pay.

It seems clear that Thompson was first hired during the time when Chorpenning's contract was annulled and before it was reinstated.[3]

Logically, either one or both postmasters had to have hired Thompson in order to keep the mail delivery schedule.

In Chapter 3, it is documented that the postmaster in Placerville first hired Thompson. Payment was discussed with the Placerville postmaster, named A. M. Thatcher.

> *The people in Utah will certainly be glad to hear about you. They are the ones petitioning the government for something to be done about being snowed in for six months of the year. So, Mr. Thompson, you have to see the postmaster in Genoa about your pay. Is that all right?*

Thompson replied: "That is good enough for me. I believe if I do my job—get Uncle Sam's mail to the people—he will pay me."

When Thompson was preparing to leave Genoa for his return trip to Placerville, Genoa postmaster S. A. Kinsey brought up the subject of payment. Kinsey said:

> *There isn't a man in this territory who wouldn't gladly help pay you for this service which will*

John A. "Snowshoe" Thompson
Pioneer Mail Carrier of the Sierra

keep us in contact with the rest of the world. Why, we not only feel buried in this snow every winter, but we feel that no one cares that we are buried. Yes, everyone here will appreciate this service; but you see, it is the business of the United States government to take care of it. As it now stands, on Aug. 18, 1856, Congress approved a post road from Placerville to Genoa, but a contract [to Chorpenning] has to be let before a carrier can collect a salary.

In a letter to the United States Senate, S. A. Kinsey said:

The mail from Placerville to this office is carried by J. A. Thompson, who travels on snowshoes, and carries the mail on his back ninety miles and for his labor charges one dollar per letter each way, which most citizens are willing to pay. Some decline to pay the dollar, and demand their letter, because they came in the United States mail.[4]

Now, there are more questions; how were these charges for mail delivery collected, and who collected them? Thompson delivered the mail to the post office, the post office gave it to the people as

Snowshoe Thompson Was Never Paid... Or Was He?

they came into the post office to get their mail. Did the postmaster collect the dollar as people picked up their mail?*

It would appear that when congress let the contract, the carrier was to be paid by the holder of the contract. The last sentence in the above quote expressed Kinsey's attempt to collect the money. Did the postmaster then pay Thompson? There will be more on this subject later in this study.

So, on what authority did either postmaster hire Thompson for this mail run? It was understood that the Post Office Department would not pay both the contractor and at the same time pay Thompson to deliver mail.

That would indicate that the mail carrier (Thompson) worked for the contractor (Chorpenning, in this case) or any others who would hold the contract to deliver mail.

Dan De Quille described the payment situation:

> *Snowshoe Thompson was one of those unfortunate persons whose lot in life it is to do a great deal of work and endure many hardships for very little pay. For twenty winters he carried the mail across the Sierra Nevada Mountains* [sic], *at times when they could have been transported in no other way than on snowshoes. After he*

---

* In 1855, the Post Office Department made pre-payment of postage a requirement. See Appendix L.

John A. "Snowshoe" Thompson
Pioneer Mail Carrier of the Sierra

began the business, he made his home in the mountains, having secured a ranch in Diamond Valley, when for five winters in succession he was constantly engaged in carrying the mail across the snowy range. Two years he carried the United States mails when there was no contract for that service and he got nothing. On both sides of the mountains he was told that an appropriation would be made and all would come out right with him; but he got nothing but promises.

When Chorpenning had the contract for carrying the mails, Thompson turned out with the oxen from his ranch and kept the roads open for a long time; when there at last came such a depth of snow that the road could no longer be broken, he mounted his snow-shoes and carried the mails on his back. Chorpenning failed, and Thompson never received a dime for his work.

Thompson took pride in the work, it challenged the spirit of adventure within him. It was like going forth to battle, and each successive trip was a victory. This being his feeling, he was all the more readily made to believe that in case he turned out and did the work, he would eventually be paid. As Mr. Thompson approached

SNOWSHOE THOMPSON WAS NEVER PAID... OR WAS HE?

his fiftieth year, he began to think that in his old age he ought to receive something from the government in reward of the services he performed. He asked but $6000 for all he had done and endured during twenty years. His petition to Congress was signed by all the State and other officials at Carson City, and every one else that was asked to sign it. In the winter of 1874 [1872], he himself went to Washington to look after his claim, but all he got was promises. He never got anything.[5]

John M. Townley offered another analysis of the situation:[6]

> *Late in 1858, Chorpenning also attempted to dispel the prevalent attitude among Congressmen and the postmaster general that scheduled service was impossible over the Sierra Nevada in the winter. Accordingly, he negotiated a $2000 contract with John A. "Snowshoe" Thompson to maintain the road through the Genoa-Placerville passes. Thompson, a long time associate of Chorpenning, had carried the mail to Carson Valley between 1854 [1856]* to 1858.*

---

* Either this is a misprint, or the date Townley used was in error as the correct date is 1856.

John A. "Snowshoe" Thompson
Pioneer Mail Carrier of the Sierra

> In 1858–1859, he used sleighs and snowplows and to conduct regular and weekly crossings of the Sierra Nevada. When storms closed the passes to sleighs, ski couriers carried the mail across the mountains.

There seemed to be no misunderstanding that Thompson was working for Chorpenning. Nonetheless, nothing has been found in any documents that would prove or disprove that Chorpenning paid Thompson. Thompson's appeal to congress for pay is described in the CVHS publication:

> In 1869, after 13 years with no compensation from the federal government,* the Nevada Legislature sent a resolution to Washington, D.C. asking for "six thousand dollars to compensate J. A. Thompson for carrying the "United States Mail" (during, 1856, 1857, and 1858).† This request was ignored by Congress.
>
> The only money Snowshoe ever received for his service was payment given him by people sending letters, for delivering letters or for delivering items he had purchased for them in Placerville. Some people paid him

---

* Apparently Thompson was not working for the federal government. But he was employed by Chorpenning, as it was Chorpenning who held the contract to deliver the mail.

† After 1858, Chorpenning no longer held the mail contract.

Snowshoe Thompson Was Never Paid...
Or Was He?

small amounts for his service but others did not. Thompson never refused to carry the mail or purchase items for anyone, whether they paid or not.[7]

So who promoted the petition to congress? The CVHS publication, *Snowshoe Thompson*, states it was the Nevada State Legislature. De Quille wrote that it was Thompson who petitioned congress.

This letter from the postmaster general supports the Nevada State legislation.

Post Office Department,
February 17, 1872
Hon. Alex. Ramsey of Minnesota
Chairman, Com. Post Offices and
Post Roads, Senate

Sir:
I have received for the Senate Committee on Post Offices and Post Roads the papers, consisting of a resolution of the State Legislature of Nevada, adopted February 4, 1869, asking for an appropriation by Congress, of $6000, "to compensate J. A. Thompson for carrying the United States Mail from Placerville, Cal., to Carson Valley, Utah, during the years 1856, 1857, and 1858," and the affidavits of A. W. Thatcher, late postmaster at Placerville, and S. A.

John A. "Snowshoe" Thompson
Pioneer Mail Carrier of the Sierra

Kinsey, late postmaster at Carson Valley, that the service was performed; and in compliance with the request that the committee be furnished with such information as the department possesses in regard to the matter, the following statement of facts, gathered from the books and files, is submitted.

The office of Carson Valley [afterwards changed to Genoa] was established July 16, 1853, as Special; that is, to be supplied with the mail under the provision of the 4th Section of the Act of March 3, 1825, the carrier receive his compensation "all the postage arising on the letters, newspapers, etc., conveyed."

This was the only condition on which the office could be opened, as there was no post road created by law to, or by, the locality. The postmaster was authorized December 13, 1854, to employ a carrier to convey the mail to and from Placerville, once a month on these terms, but the sum paid not to exceed $250 a year. It appears by the postmaster's return, in the Auditor's office, that he employed J. A. Thompson, and paid him postages collected as follows:

SNOWSHOE THOMPSON WAS NEVER PAID...
OR WAS HE?

1st quarter, 1856
(January 1 to March 31) $15.39
4th quarter, 1856
(October 1 to December 31)   8.00
Total, 1856 $23.39
1st quarter 1857   21.74
4th quarter 1857   35.09
Total, 1857 $56.83
[Total both years] $80.22

Interruption of this interesting letter is necessary to make this observation: The first mail delivery contract for Absalom Woodward and George Chorpenning was issued in 1851 on Post Route 5066. Why did the postmaster general state "...there was no post road created by law to, or by, the locality," when in fact there was.*[8]

From the above accounting, it does appear that the postmaster in Genoa paid Thompson for the winters of 1856 and 1857. However, from De Quille's interview, Thompson states he "was not paid a dime."

Continuing with the postmaster general's letter:

> It seems by these returns that no mails were received at the office

---

* The postmaster general signed the certification attesting to the "true and correct copies, first, of a contract between Geo. Chorpenning and the Post Office Department for caring the mail on route No. 5066, from Sacramento City to Salt Lake City, signed April 25th, 1851..." A second document stated that copy of said contract was to be placed on file that "...can now be found on the files of the Post Office Department." Signed by Second Assistant Postmaster General. By this time Woodard had died, so Chorpenning was the only claimant.

John A. "Snowshoe" Thompson
Pioneer Mail Carrier of the Sierra

during the 2nd and 3rd quarters of these years; and that this is correct with reference to the third quarter of 1856, is shown by a letter from the postmaster dated August 11 of that year, in which he states that "what mails we send or receive is taken gratis by whoever is traveling to and fro." With regard to year 1858, the records show that Thompson could have carried no mails during that year.

However, from Chapter 7, Thompson was still delivering mail in 1858, 1859, and for years to follow. Is it possible that Thompson was delivering mail out of his sense of civic duty for no pay?

The letter continues:

> *In the Act of Congress "to establish certain post roads," approved August 18, 1856, the road from Placerville to Genoa, was included as a post road and on 15th January, 1857, mail service on it was invited by advertisement, with other routes, from September 1, 1857, to June 30, 1858. This resulted in a contract with J. B. Crandell, for weekly trips, for the time mentioned, at a rate of $1800 per annum; this contract was faithfully carried out, and said contractor paid in full.*

Snowshoe Thompson Was Never Paid... Or Was He?

> From July 1, 1858, the route was covered by the contract of George Chorpenning, from Salt Lake to Placerville, and service was continued under other contracts until it was superseded by the opening of the Central Pacific Railroad. Thompson cannot, therefore, lay claims to any service in 1858, and to but two quarters in each of the years 1856 and 1857; and, in fact, one in 1857, (the 4th), which he was paid $35.09, was included in the contract with Crandell.

Further light on the subject is thrown by two letters from postmaster S. A. Kinsey, of Carson Valley, found on file. As mentioned earlier, in one dated December 26, 1856, he says:

> The mail from Placerville is carried by J. A. Thompson, who travels on snow-shoes, and carries the mail on his back, ninety miles, and for his labor charges one dollar per letter each way, which most of the citizens are willing to pay: some decline to pay the dollar, and demand their letters because they come in the U.S. mail;

He then he asks instructions as to the disposition of such letters. On 1st of January, 1857, he writes as follows:

John A. "Snowshoe" Thompson
Pioneer Mail Carrier of the Sierra

> *The lowest sum for which this office can be supplied with mail, monthly, or semi-monthly, from Placerville, is $1000. J. A. Thompson will carry it for that sum. He is a man that I can recommend. He has carried the mail for the past two winters, and is carrying it now, and he charges one dollar per letter each way.*
>
> *The mail is carried over the Sierra Nevada mountains [sic], 90 miles; six months in the year it is carried on the carrier's back, and he travels on snowshoes.*

From this detail it is difficult to determine the exact amount of mail service performed by this individual, its value to the community, and the amount of his claim, if any, on the United States for remuneration. The only service clearly shown to have been rendered is for the two quarters in each of the years 1856 and 1857, and from the latter year should be taken the fourth quarter, which was covered by contract to another party [J. B. Crandell].

> *Three-fourths of a year may, therefore, be considered as the extent of his services, which at $1000, the amount named as Thompson's price by the postmaster at Carson Valley, amounts to $750.00, from which deduct the aggregate of four payments by the postmaster, $82.22—Balance, $669.78*

Snowshoe Thompson Was Never Paid... Or Was He?

> *—Saying nothing of the "one dollar per letter" which is stated he charged to individuals, and is presumed to be correspondence carried out of the mails. The papers submitted, three in number, are herewith returned.*
> *Very respectfully,*
> *Your obedient servant,*
> *John A. J. Creswell,*
> *Postmaster General*[9]

So, does this letter "prove" that Snowshoe Thompson was paid for his services, or is Postmaster General Creswell just verifying the amount Thompson should have been paid?

Assume for a moment that Thompson was paid the $669.78, even though there is no documentation to support this assumption. It definitely was not the $6,000 Thompson was seeking, nor the amount supported by the Nevada State Legislature. It is important to note that this letter was dated 1872, concerning deliveries for 1856, 1857, and 1858.

After 1858 and into the early 1870s, Thompson continued his mail deliveries as later documentation would illustrate. That brings up a new question concerning the contractor: who employed Thompson in those intervening years?

George Chorpenning, upon receiving a third contract to deliver mail, best described the history of his contracts in his May 1, 1874, petition to the U.S. Court of claims titled, "A Brief History of the Facts by the Claimant."[10]

John A. "Snowshoe" Thompson
Pioneer Mail Carrier of the Sierra

> *Meanwhile, as my second contract was about to expire, in April 1858, I entered into a third contract.*
>
> *This was to carry the mails between Salt Lake City and Placerville, California, in four horse coaches, weekly each way, through twelve days commencing July 1, 1858 and ending June 30, 1862, at a compensation, especially agreed upon with the Postmaster General Brown, of $190,000 per annum.*
>
> *This, with a contract made at the same time with J. M. Hockaday & Co. for a similar service, at about $200,000, from St. Joseph, Missouri, to Salt Lake, through in twenty days, formed the first overland stage line ever established across the plains.*[11]

Running a stagecoach with mail and passengers was a major and expensive undertaking for Chorpenning. As usual, he found great difficulty meeting his delivery schedules, especially during the winter months over the Sierra.

Chapter 7 verifies Thompson's role in keeping the road open during the winter. This had to be a great aide to Chorpenning, and there must have been some compensation coming to Thompson from Chorpenning. A different perspective of the situation is presented in this article:

Snowshoe Thompson Was Never Paid... Or Was He?

Sacramento Union
December 10, 1858

    Notwithstanding the snow that fell last week, the mail came through from Carson Valley, and was followed immediately by the coach. The storm must have been a severe one, as more snow fell at Placerville, Diamond Springs, etc., than is usually seen at these points. But we regret to hear that there has been some misunderstanding between the mail contractor and Thompson, the former mountain expressman,* who contracted to keep the road free of snow obstruction during the winter.
    In consequence of neglect on the part of the contractor to comply with his portion of the agreement, Thompson, we hear, abandoned the road, and has gone to his ranch in the Valley.
    This is a bad blunder on the part of the contractor, and will probably cause him a good deal of trouble. We do not hear anything further by this mail of the new coaches and additional mules, reported to have arrived at Salt Lake

---

* The use of the word "former," if true, could support the postmaster general's statement earlier that Thompson did not deliver the mail during the year 1858.

John A. "Snowshoe" Thompson
Pioneer Mail Carrier of the Sierra

for Chorpenning. It was understood that they would be immediately placed upon the line.[12]

Business for Chorpenning was beginning to unravel as he described his last days as a mail contractor and his growing frustrations over the years.

But I was wedded to my project and had no idea of what was going on in the department or outside to crush me. I knew very well, as every one did, that soon there must be a daily mail over that route, and to that I was looking with bright hopes from the day I started with the first mail, in May, 1851, when finally, without a single intimation from the department of dissatisfaction in regard to the character of the work or the manner in which it was being performed—without any complaint or notice whereby I could have corrected the error, had any existed, and have met my conspirators or accusers and made a defense—my contract, on 25th of May, 1856, was annulled...I had now been carrying that mail nearly an entire year since my pay had been cut down, without receiving from the department a single dollar for the work done during that time.[13]

Chorpenning experienced this pattern with all three of his contracts, eventually receiving a

Snowshoe Thompson Was Never Paid... Or Was He?

settlement, but not until after 1876. How much Chorpenning had to pay for his numerous travels to Washington, D.C., lawyer fees, and court costs will most likely remain a mystery. The same questions appear repeatedly as to why Thompson would not have received any pay from Chorpenning, to say nothing about those others who were in his employ.

However, the story of Thompson's mail delivery service and another contractor who would be awarded Chorpenning's route did not end there. Chapter 4 reported that when Chorpenning's last contract was annulled in 1860, the contract was awarded to William Russell.

There is another rather complex story concerning how Thompson might have fit into the mail delivery system. It is a known fact that Thompson continued to deliver mail into the 1870s, but what is not known, is why he was not paid after Chorpenning's contract was annulled. That is assuming that those holding the mail delivery contracts after Chorpenning would want and need the services of Thompson during the winter.

Trying to follow what happened when William Russell was awarded the mail contract in 1860 has been equally complex.

The story of William H. Russell, Alexander Majors, William B. Waddell, and their business adventures is also very complicated, involving other partners and other endeavors. Some background history may help in understanding this study. On January 10, 1855, the firm of Russell, Majors, and Waddell was organized[14] and would become one of the largest freighting companies in the country. On

John A. "Snowshoe" Thompson
Pioneer Mail Carrier of the Sierra

March 27, 1855, the largest single contract ever let up to that time by the Quartermaster's Department at Fort Leavenworth, Kansas, went up for bid, under a Major Sibley, for transportation of 50,000 to 2,500,000 pounds of military stores from Fort Leavenworth to Fort Union, located near Salt Lake City, and intermediary points.[15]

This contract would require huge numbers of wagons, men, and animals.

In 1859, Horace Greeley wrote about the Russell, Majors, and Waddell Company:

> *Russell, Majors and Waddell's transportation establishment is a great feature of Leavenworth. Such acres of wagons! such pyramids of extra axletrees! such herds of oxen! such regiments of drivers and other employees! No one who does not see can realize how vast a business this is, nor immense its outlays as well as its income. I presume this great firm has at this hour two millions of dollars invested in stock, mainly oxen, mules and wagons. (They last year employed six thousand teamsters and worked 45,000 oxen).*[16]

What is important to this study is to note that this company picked up the mail contract from Fort Leavenworth to Salt Lake City and on into California. Chorpenning's contract was annulled in 1860. As mentioned many times before, in 1860 and 1861,

SNOWSHOE THOMPSON WAS NEVER PAID...
OR WAS HE?

the Pony Express entered the picture, and "came-and-went" when the transcontinental telegraph was completed.

Where did that leave Thompson? It looks as if he played an insignificant part in that very large enterprise. By the end of 1859, Russell, Majors, and Waddell were deep in debt and on the verge of being bankrupt.*[17] Russell, however, was relying on the $600,000 per-annum mail delivery contract between Leavenworth and California that still had two years remaining to keep the business going.[18]

In January of 1860, Russell began a huge undertaking: building 190 relay stations, purchasing four hundred horses, hiring station tenders, and hiring eighty pony riders, all of which had to be, essentially, operational in sixty-five days.[19]

On April 3, 1860, the first pony riders departed from eastern and western stations at the same time† on the first commercial express mail delivery adventure in American history. The Pony Express would encounter numerous problems—weather, terrain, Indian issues, worry over problems between the North and the South—along with the competition of the nearly completed transcontinental telegraph.

In the story previously told, not only was the Williams Station burned at the beginning of the Paiute War, but also other stations. This would not only affect the Russell, Majors, and Waddell

---

* For a more complete accounting of their business, endeavors, and financial difficulties read *War Drums and Wagon Wheels: The Story of Russell, Majors, and Waddell* by Raymond Settle.
† The Pony Express riders left simultaneously with their mailbag (*mochila*) at either end of the trail, one from St. Joseph, Missouri, and one from Sacramento, California.

John A. "Snowshoe" Thompson
Pioneer Mail Carrier of the Sierra

partnership, but our friend, John "Snowshoe" Thompson's life, as well.

As far as getting the mail to its intended destinations in ten days, the Pony Express was a success; financially it was a disaster. The completion of the telegraph was the main reason the Pony Express was no longer needed as news and communications could be received in only the time it took to tap the message.

Operational costs of the Pony Express venture were exorbitant. The cost for a one-ounce letter was five dollars or about $135 in 2015 dollars. Therefore only businesses and newspapers could afford the enormous charge.[20]

The basic cost for operating the Pony Express was $1,000 per day. The company was showing expenditures of $700,000, with receipts of $500,000.[21] Russell, who was the major force behind the Pony Express, was forced to resign, and the enterprise went bankrupt.[22] An assumption could be made that if Thompson had worked for Russell, Majors, and Waddell, they did not pay him because of their financial problems. It seemed a reoccurring theme with mail contracts, does it not?

However, newspaper accounts reported that Thompson was still delivering mail for years to come. As related in Chapter 7, in 1871 it was reported that Thompson returned home to Silver Mountain City from delivering the mail to find his son, Arthur, ill.

Mentioned earlier in this chapter, Thompson petitioned congress for $6,000 for back pay, only to have his request ignored. At the encouragement of his friends, Thompson set out for Washington, D.C.

Snowshoe Thompson Was Never Paid... Or Was He?

in 1874, to confer with anyone who would listen to his request.

Dan De Quille described this trip as told to him by Thompson:

> When Thompson went to Washington in 1874 [1872],* he left Reno, Nevada, January 17th. Three days afterwards the train got stuck in a big snow-drift, thirty five miles this side of Laramie [Wyoming]. There it stuck, in spite of the efforts of four locomotives to pull it through, preceded by a full day's shoveling by all the men that could be pressed into service.
>
> It was on Sunday that the four engines were tried and "found wanting." On Monday morning the wind was still blowing a gale, and the snow was still drifting badly.
>
> Becoming impatient, Thompson, with one fellow passenger—Rufus Turner, of Idaho—set out on foot and walked to Laramie, where they overtook a train that was also stuck fast in the snow a short distance outside the village. At Laramie, Turner came to the conclusion that he wanted no more pedestrian exercise,

---

* De Quille's date is incorrect. The following letters from Washington, D.C., written by Thompson to his wife are dated 1872.

John A. "Snowshoe" Thompson
Pioneer Mail Carrier of the Sierra

with the thermometer ranging at from fifteen to thirty degrees below zero.

Thompson, however, was not daunted. He pushed on alone. He walked two days, fifty-six miles further, which carried him to Cheyenne [Wyoming], he having spent the intervening night in Buford Station, near the summit.

At Cheyenne he found a train just starting out, and boarding it, went through to the Missouri River— the first man directly from the Pacific Coast for about two weeks. At the time, the newspapers in the East gave Mr. Thompson great credit for his achievement, declaring he was the first man who had ever beaten the "iron horse" on so long a stretch.[23]

These two letters that Thompson wrote to Agnes, setting aside his misspelling and punctuation, best described his time spent in Washington, D. C.

Washington, D.C. Feb. 6, 1872

Dear Wife,

I arrived here last Friday the 2nd I wrote you a few lines from Ogden and also from Laramie and Telegraphed you from Chianene I got to Pittsburg [Pennsylvania] last Monday and Staid

Snowshoe Thompson Was Never Paid...
Or Was He?

there two days with Delorma he was very glad to See me and Said I was mutch younger looking then he expected to See me from the likeness I Sent him. Mr and Mrs Harbaugh his uncle and aunt lives in the grandest Stile they live 4 miles out from the Business portion of the City in a large Brick Munsion wich is furnished with the richest furniture through out that money can buy Mrs Harbaugh has a fine Carrage and a Black Servant at her command and Delorma has a fine Horse and Buggy to him Self he rides in to town evry morning to the office where he keeps Books for Mr. Harbaugh as he has a large mill for roling Rail Road Iron. They had Delorma to take me in his Buggy all over the City and Showed me the iron roling mills and the glass Factory museum and other places of interest

The prices for all of most everything is higher here then back there They Charge 21 Dollars per week here at the Hotels for board and a Single room I have hired a room for 4 Dollars per week and I take meals at restaurants at a Dollar a day for two meals. I asked the price of a pair of gaiter Shoes today they Said I could have them for 11 Dollars It gave me

John A. "Snowshoe" Thompson
Pioneer Mail Carrier of the Sierra

Such a Scare that I dared not aske of a pair of Boots So I ware my Buffalos yet
  Senetor Ney of Nevada called for my papers from the Committee and they may find them in a day or two. The law making here goes very Slow Friday and Saturday the Senate was not in Session and yesterday And to day they were debating on the everlasting Negro Question.
  I have found Some warm friends from California who Says they will help me all they can the whether has bin Stormy most of the time last Sunday it Snowed 5 inches and to day it has bin raining
  My love to all From your Affectionate Husband
  J. A. Thompson

And the second letter,

Washington, D.C. March 7, 1872
Dear Wife,

  I am still in this City and in good health But my business gos Slow I got the first hearing today before the Committee. I appeared before them myself and I had all so a man by the name of Bee from Placerville as witness. Senetor Nye was allso before the Committee.

Snowshoe Thompson Was Never Paid... Or Was He?

I Sapose the committee will make a report in a few days either for or against me. I think as Soon as they report I shal Start for home for if they report against me it will be no use to try any more and if it is for me, it will take two or three mounths before it will get through both houses. I think they will alow me Something but will cut the amount down.

Mr Harbaugh was here last week and he done all he could for me. He knowed great many of the members of Congress.

I am now living at a Boarding House where I pay ten dollars a week. I have a large room all to my Self well furnished. It has bin very cold hear this week. In New York there has bin three person froze to death one man was found in his wagon holding the reins and was froze Stif the horses was walking along.

If it is fine wether the last week in march or first of Aprile the Boys had better go to Plowing and Sowing the driest ground. Send that red plow down to Genoa and get it fixed in good order and you had better Send down to Johnsons and buy an other good Steel Plow.

Arthur you must be a good Boy and mind what Mother and

John A. "Snowshoe" Thompson
Pioneer Mail Carrier of the Sierra

Grandmother tels you then I will be So Pleased when I cum home and have them tell me all about how good you have bin.
Husband, J. A. Thompson[24]

Following is the report from the Senate Committee on Post Offices and Post Roads regarding Thompson's request for payment of services. Much of the report is background information that has been previously described, nevertheless it is deemed essential to provide the report in its entirety to bring together all elements as regards to the final decision.

42D Congress 2d session
SENATE   Report No. 73
March 14, 1872
Ordered to be printed

Mr. Kelly made the following REPORT:
[To accompany Bill S. 806]
The Committee on Post-Offices and Post-Roads, to whom was referred the resolution of the State of Nevada asking for an appropriation of six thousand dollars to compensate J. A. Thompson for carrying the United States mail from Placerville, California, to Carson Valley, in Utah Territory, report as follows;
On 16th of July, 1853 the post-office of Carson Valley was established as special; that is, to be supplied with

Snowshoe Thompson Was Never Paid... Or Was He?

the mail under provisions of the 4th section of the act of March 3, 1825, the carrier to receive as his compensation, "all the postage arising on letters, newspapers, &c., conveyed." There was no post-road to Carson Valley until one was established by the act of Congress approved August 18, 1856, from Placerville, in California, to Genoa, in Utah; and no provision for carrying the mails thereon until September, 1857, when J. B. Crandell commenced to carry them under contract with the Post-Office Department.*

During the winter if 1856 and 1857, while the people residing east of the Sierra Nevada Mountains [sic] were cut off from all communication with California, the claimant, J. A. Thompson, undertook and did carry the mails from Placerville to Carson Valley, a distance of ninety miles.

Twice a month with regularity he performed the perilous journey over the Sierra Nevada Mountains [sic], traveling on snow-shoes, with a mail averaging forty pounds on his back. For a distance of sixty miles there was no habitation on the way, and all traces of the road were obliterated by snow

---

* It is curious to note there was no mention of Chorpenning's contract, and nothing of the Post Route No. 5066, Placerville to Salt Lake City, established in 1851.

John A. "Snowshoe" Thompson
Pioneer Mail Carrier of the Sierra

from fifteen to twenty feet deep; and all travel obstructed for five or six months in the year. No person save Thompson could be found who was willing, under these circumstances, to transport the mails across the mountains; and he was indeed to do it only by the urgent solicitation of the people of Carson Valley, and the hope that in the future he might be paid for his services.

On the 1st of January, 1857, the postmaster at Carson Valley wrote to the Post-Office Department that the lowest sum for which that office could be supplied with the mail, monthly or semi-monthly, from Placerville, was $1000, and that J. A. Thompson was willing to carry it for that amount; and recommend him as a proper man to perform the service. At that same time he stated that Thompson was then carrying the mail, and charged $1 per letter each way. It appeared, however, from the evidence before the committee, that Thompson received but little, if anything, from this source, as letters were deposited in the post office, and most persons to whom they were addressed demanded and received them without payment of $1 per letter, which the postmaster tried to secure for the carrier as a compensation for his services.

SNOWSHOE THOMPSON WAS NEVER PAID... OR WAS HE?

By reference to a letter of the Postmaster General to the chairman of the Committee on Post-Offices and Post-Roads, dated February 17, 1872, and which is hereto attached,* it appears that Thompson carried the mails two quarters in the year 1856 and two in the year 1857, although the latter quarter, in the year 1857, was during the time that contract was awarded to J. B. Crandell. He (Crandell) was fully paid by the United States government for that quarter, although it seems he failed to pay Thompson, who performed the service for him.

It further appears, by the postmaster's returns in the Auditor's Office that he paid Thompson, postage collected at the office, the sum of $80.22; and so far as the evidence goes, this seems to be full amount of money he has received for his service.

The committee therefore recommends that J. A. Thompson be paid for three-fourth of a year service in carrying the mails, at a rate of $1000 per annum, making the sum $750, from which is to be deducted $80.22 already paid, leaving the sum $669.78 still due.[25]

---

* This letter is printed earlier in this chapter.

John A. "Snowshoe" Thompson
Pioneer Mail Carrier of the Sierra

Was this recommendation to congress for pay to Thompson ever brought to a vote and passed? Perhaps the answer can be found in the following letters. In 1992, Melbourne Z. Myerson, president of the El Dorado County Historical Society, wrote to Congressman John Doolittle from California, requesting any information on the subject of Thompson's pay. Following are excerpts from the letter, dated June 30, 1992:

> *Dear Mr. Doolittle,*
>
> *I want to thank your office for assisting me so promptly in obtaining information from the Library of Congress relative to John A. "Snowshoe" Thompson...*
>
> *Specifically, I require a copy of Senate Report 73, printed March 14, 1872, which was to accompany S. 806, and a copy of any Senate proceedings related to S. 806, which I assume might be found in the Congressional Globe for that era. This all took place in the 42nd Congress, 2nd Session in 1872. The Report 73 indicated the Committee on Post Office and Post roads recommended that Thompson be paid $669.78 for his efforts to carry the mail across the Sierra Nevada during the first and fourth quarters of 1856 and the first and fourth quarters of 1857.*
>
> *Historians have generally taken*

Snowshoe Thompson Was Never Paid... Or Was He?

the position that Thompson had never been paid for his 20 years of work, and I find it difficult to believe any hardy soul such as Thompson would merrily go along all those back-breaking years hoping that a beneficent Congress might pay him one day. That is not realistic...
Sincerely,
Melbourne Z. Myerson

Two letters from Megaera Harris, Historian for Corporate Information Services, respond to Mr. Myerson on U. S. Postal Service letterhead. Here are some excerpts taken from one of those letters:

November 3, 1992

Dear Mr. Myerson,
Thank you for your recent letter noting that Congress authorized payment to John A. Thompson for carrying the mail across the Sierra Nevada Mountains [sic] in the 1850's and requesting information verifying payment by the Postmaster General of this service.
I have enclosed a copy of Report Number 73, dated March 14, 1872... On December 10, 1872, Senate Bill 806 was referred to the House for approval. On February 4, 1873, the House referred the bill to the committee on

John A. "Snowshoe" Thompson
Pioneer Mail Carrier of the Sierra

claims, but the bill apparently was never enacted into law. Another bill (H.R. 974, 43rd Congress, 1st Session) was introduced in 1874, referred to the Committee on Claims, but apparently never passed. Unfortunately, I have no information on why these bills were not enacted.

Regarding the contract won by J. B. Crandell for $1800, postal mail route records at the National Archives and Records Administration show that Thompson had submitted a bid for $2000 for service "on Norwegian Snowskates from December to April and on horseback the remainder of the year." If Thompson was subcontracted as a mail carrier for Crandell, his claim would have been against Crandell rather than the Post Office.

Later records indicate that John A. Thompson, of Silver Mountain, California, was regularly designated by the Post Office Department as the contractor on Route 14763, from Genoa to Silver Mountain, from July 1, 1870, though June 30 1874, at $1856 per annum. There is no indication in the records that Mr. Thompson was not compensated for his service... .

*Sincerely,
Megaera Harris, Historian
Corporate Information Services*[26]

Snowshoe Thompson Was Never Paid... Or Was He?

Here are excerpts from the other letter:

November 30, 1992

Dear Mr. Myerson,

Thank you for your letter of November 7, 1992.

In response to your two questions: Was Snowshoe Thompson paid $669.78 by an Act of Congress?

No. It is true that the Senate passed a bill on December 10, 1872, directing the Post Master General to pay John A. Thompson the sum of $669.78. On the same day, the bill was referred to the house for approval. On February 4, 1873, the House referred the bill to the Committee on Claims, but we have no record of the bill being enacted into law. Another bill (H.R. 974, 43rd Congress, 1st Session) was introduced in 1874, again referred to the House Committee on Claims, and again not passed.

In line with this question, you indicated that you disagree that the Post Office Department had no responsibility to pay a subcontractor or employee.

I contacted our General Counsel's office, which confirmed that

John A. "Snowshoe" Thompson
Pioneer Mail Carrier of the Sierra

> *the contractor, not the Postal Service or former Post Office Department, is responsible for payment to the contractor's employees... .*
>
> *Sincerely,*
> *Megaera Harris,*
> *Historian Corporate Information Services*[27]

It appears that Thompson did receive payments of $80.22 for his mail delivery services, and possibly $1,856 for his Genoa to Silver Mountain contract. It is most interesting in the first letter Harris stated, "There is no indication in the records that Mr. Thompson was not compensated for his services."

Back to square one? Until documents appear to the contrary, it must be assumed that Crandell did not pay him.

This study shows some possible misrepresentation of the truth by the postmaster general to Thompson. Contradictions surface as to when, or if, Thompson was delivering mail in 1858. It is clear that he was a victim of circumstances.

There is a strong belief that when Thompson first applied for the position to deliver mail in the winter in 1855, his motivation was not solely money. The job offered Thompson a challenge and an opportunity to provide the much needed mail delivery over the Sierra in the winter, utilizing a skill he had to provide that service.

He may have been naive in believing that the Post Office Department would honor their commitment, and his performance of that

Snowshoe Thompson Was Never Paid...
Or Was He?

commitment. Remember, when the postmaster in Placerville told Thompson he would get his pay from the postmaster in Genoa, Thompson had remarked, "That is good enough for me. I believe if I do my job—get Uncle Sam's mail to the people—he will pay me."

Thompson was an honorable man who expected others to be honorable as well. When the mail delivery contractors hired Thompson, he most likely assumed he would be paid. In regards to the mail contractors, Thompson was once again a victim. With Chorpenning underbidding on all his contracts, causing him constant financial trouble, his not paying Thompson was just collateral damage.

Regardless of all of the documents, research, speculations, and assumptions, most would have to agree that Thompson was never paid enough for his twenty years of dedicated service.

John A. "Snowshoe" Thompson
Pioneer Mail Carrier of the Sierra

10

Thompson's Last Years

John A. Thompson served on the Alpine County Board of Supervisors from 1868 to 1872. In 1871, he was a delegate to the Republican State Convention in Sacramento.[1]

He was appointed sub-Indian agent to the Walker River Indians in 1857, as stated in Chapter 6. It became obvious that he had an interest in the political arena, including his 1859 appointment as a Notary Public by the governor of Utah Territory.

It is logical that when Alpine County was established in 1864,[2] Thompson would keep a close watch over the development of the young county in which he lived and owned property. In 1867, Thompson tossed his hat into the political ring when he ran for Alpine County Assessor against W. P. Merrill, and lost by a count of 160 to 116.[3] His defeat did not deter him from running for another office.

In the Alpine County election for the Board

THOMPSON'S LAST YEARS

of Supervisors of November 3, 1868, his name appeared on the ballot with four other candidates for Supervisory District 1. The board minutes do not list the results of the election; however, at the next board meeting of January 4, 1869, the minutes stated that board member John Thompson was present for that meeting.[4] The Board of Supervisors minutes of May 4, July 8, and August 9, 1869, stated that J. A. Thompson was paid seven dollars for one day's salary and mileage, along with reflecting payments to another two members of the board.[5]

An interesting entry appeared as an agenda item in the August 9, 1869, board minutes. "In the matter of J. A. Thompson resignation from Supervisor District 1. The resignation of J. A. Thompson is read and accepted and ordered to the file. The county clerk is ordered to call an election to fill the vacancy caused by such resignation."[6]

The Alpine County Board of Supervisors office was located in what was then the county seat, Silver Mountain City. Minutes dated September 6, 1869, gave the election returns from the September 1, 1869, election, declaring J. A. Thompson the winner in Supervisory District 2, defeating W. Clogeton fifty-five votes to thirty-one.[7] It is not clear from the board minutes what events took place that caused Thompson to resign from District 1 and then run for election from District 2 the following month.

The Alpine County tax records for 1867, documented in Chapter 7, show that Thompson was assessed for property he owned at Silver Mountain

John A. "Snowshoe" Thompson
Pioneer Mail Carrier of the Sierra

City (Alpine County Seat and Supervisory District 1) and for his home on 160 acres in Diamond Valley (Supervisor District 2). It could be speculated that Thompson needed to declare the site of his primary residence, and he simply chose Diamond Valley. Nonetheless, Thompson was again voted to serve as a member of the Alpine County Board of Supervisors. He was very active as a member of the board and attended nearly every meeting; often there were only two supervisors present to conduct business.

During this time, the Alpine County Board of Supervisors also served as the Alpine County Board of Equalization. Their job was to determine the assessed value of the land and set the tax rate, set the fees for many toll roads in the county, and to set the salary for the supervisors. Thompson was a very active member in those processes. It seemed, from the numerous entries in the minutes of those meetings, Thompson, along with the property owners, testified regarding the assessed value.

Other board members also testified regarding tax increases,[8] as increasing taxes was a regular practice of the board. In most cases, the board raised the taxes of the property owner. In one case, where Thompson testified, the taxes were raised from two hundred dollars to four hundred dollars, and in another the taxes were raised from $1,500 to $2,500. By March 20, 1870, he was making fourteen dollars for one day with mileage, a raise from the seven dollars of 1869.

In the July 3, 1871, minutes, Thompson's signature appeared for the first time as Chairman of the Board of Supervisors,[9] where he served until the

Thompson's Last Years

election of November 1872. In his bid for reelection, C. B. Gregory defeated him, fifty votes to fourteen. Thompson's name appeared for the last time as member of the Board of Supervisors in the January 6, 1873, minutes when he received his final salary of sixteen dollars.[10] It could be speculated that Thompson's landslide defeat could have been due in part to his involvement with testifying for the tax increases.

Thompson would run again for public office in the September 6, 1875, election. He ran for the California State Assembly office against two other candidates. S. A. Mott defeated him in a very closely contested race with the count ninety votes to eighty-seven. This was the end of Thompson's political life. In nine months he would be dead.

Not much has been found of Thompson's contacts with his relatives in the Midwest. In this rare letter, which Thompson wrote after he returned from Washington, D.C., to his niece Christina in Minnesota, he shared a little of his thoughts and feelings about his California home. It also gives a hint that he might have been a bit sentimental and would have liked his relatives to be closer. It appeared he visited his niece on his way to or from Washington. The last time he had seen or had even heard from his relatives could have been about twenty-two years earlier.

John A. Thompson
Silver Mountain, Alpine County, Cal.
Woodfords Alpine County, Cal.
Dec. 28. 1873

John A. "Snowshoe" Thompson
Pioneer Mail Carrier of the Sierra

Dear Neice Christina and Husband,

...I received your letter of April 9th and I was glad to see that you was well and that you was not among the number that Froze to Death in your State and I think you was about right when you say that you was getting sick of Minnesota. Now in regard to government land there is none hear that is fit for cultavation but what is taken up and farms is worth $1000.00 to $10,000.00 according to size and quality.

About 200 miles from the Pacific Coast east lays a chain of mountains called the Seria Nevadas. They are on the average about 7000 feet high covered with heavy timber and the high peak has snow on them year round. On the east side of the main mountain is the State of Nevada and Utah.

The country is composed of ranges of mountains and deserets inter spiresed with small valley that is fit for cultivation if water can be found to irrigate with, but thare is not on a average more than one acre in 1000 fit to cultavate for 1500 miles. East of here the mountains is covered with brush and bunch grass which makes good runy for cattle summer and winter. Allso those mountains in full of minneral prinsable silver gold copper iron and cs. I live on the east and at the foot of the Sierra Nevada Mountains with in 3 miles of the state line of Nevada.

In the valley where I live there is 5 farms then 5 miles to the north over some hills is Carson valley. It is the largest valley east of the mountains. It is 10 miles by 20. About one half of it is fit for cultavation. We here half to irrigate all our crops as it does not rain here for 6 months in a year. We do not rase as mutch grain to the acre as they do on the west side of the mountains buyt we do get a better price for everything.

This year we did not get mutch more than half crop of grain on the count of very cold spring. We had 800 bushel of wheat and oat and 12 tons of potatoes. Grain is worth 3½ cts. per pound. Potatoes 2½ cts. per pound, hay is worth 1 cts. per pound.

The only drawback to this part of Cal. is the late frost in the spring and it comes early in the fall. So we can't raise any fruit here but currents and goos berry's. But we are blessed with warm winds during the summer. Along the west of the range to the Pacific Ocan is low hills and valleys

John A. "Snowshoe" Thompson
Pioneer Mail Carrier of the Sierra

that are very rich and are sure of a crop evry year as the foggs come in from the ocean and forms a heavy dewes night, whereas the Sacramento and San Joaquin valley of a dry season fails in crops when they have no showers after the first of March, That is away from the rivers. It is some talk of turning the rivers along the foot hills and irrigate those vast plains and if they do there will be no better country in the world.

Now I would like to have you come out here, and more of my relation, but I do not like to persuade any body to come for they may not like it, for some likes one country and some another, but as for myself I would rather be landed in California without a cent then to have the best farm in Wisconsin or Minnesota.

How mutch of a farm have you got there and can you sell it and what price. Please answer...To show you the deference between this country and Minnesota I will state that I have 90 head of cattle and 20 head of horses to winter. Half of this number is my own the rest belong to other parties living higher up in the mountains which I have taken to feed. This number of stock I expect to winter on what straw I have and about 15 tons of hay. Can you do that in Minnesota? Now I have tryed to describe the country east of the mountains.

So I will now try and describe the western slope. About 40 miles from summit commences the gold mines which stretches the hole length of the state 600 miles and 40 miles wide. The gold is about all washed from the surface but there is great many deep mines wich pays well. In this mining belt is the greatest fruit growing country in the world. All the fruit you can think of grows here in a bundance. They also rase some grain and vegetables. West of this commences state grain growing valley.

Sacramento valley extends north 200 miles and the San Joaquin 300 miles to the south and thay are about 50 miles wide. Most all good land raise from 20 to 30 bushels of wheat to the acre and 40 to 50 bushels of oats or barley...and it never snows there once in 10 years. All kinds of vegetables and fruit grow to a great size. There is a good deal of government land in these valleys but most is held under Mexican Grants. The Mexican government give to each man that wanted land from 2 to 10 miles squire. Thay sell it now from 5 to 10 dollars per acre with out improvements. West of these valley is

John A. "Snowshoe" Thompson
Pioneer Mail Carrier of the Sierra

a smaller range of mountains.
Write soon, Our best wishes for your
weelfare
                  from your uncle,
                  J. A. Thompson.[11]

Another indication that Thompson might have visited some relatives is a letter dated June 24, 1957, written by his great niece, Miss Grace Thompson, posted from Madison, Wisconsin, to an author Evelyn Dangberg Teal, who wrote *Flying Snowshoes*. Grace wrote to thank and compliment Evelyn Teal for her recently published book on Snowshoe Thompson.[12]

Grace told Evelyn what she knew about some of the Thompson family history and knew of his visit with his brother, Torstein, when he went to Washington, D.C. In her letter she wrote:

> *I have a copy of the letter John wrote to his wife while he was in Washington. He had stopped on his way there to see his brother Thostein. My father was 8 years old then but others mentioned him to us.** [13]

As time went on, and the transcontinental railroad was completed, the need for Thompson to deliver the mail in the winter diminished.† Mail

---
* Grace Thompson did seem to confuse the spellings of Torstein several times in her letter, i.e., Thostein and Tosten names, and adding Thompson Rue to his name.
† The transcontinental railroad was completed at Promontory Summit, Utah Territory, on May 13, 1869.

Thompson's Last Years

could be delivered from Sacramento to Reno, Nevada, in a day. From Reno it could be sent to Carson City and Genoa. Thompson still held the Genoa to Silver Mountain mail delivery contract, as has been dealt with in a previous chapter.

Thompson never got over "gold fever." Elma Bradshaw described his continual quest for riches, when two years after his return from Washington D.C., he found some rich ore.

> Two years passed and Snowshoe still carried the mail. While resting one day on one of his last trips for the winter season, he picked up a shining piece of rock.
>
> It was gold! Examining the place more closely, he determined that here was a rich vein of ore. He realized with great relief now that the mail contract did not matter, he would be fixed for life-financially. He rushed through the rest of his trip and quickly went back home to tell Agnes and Arthur. It was rich ore as the assayer had assured him.

Note: at the present time, nothing more has been found concerning Thompson's gold discovery and mining efforts.

Bradshaw continued,

> ...After his discovery of gold, Snowshoe settled down to farming and ranching on his place in Diamond

John A. "Snowshoe" Thompson
Pioneer Mail Carrier of the Sierra

Valley—not knowing that he had less than 2 years left to spend there with his wife and son.

His pre-death illness was brief, and though it was severe, he spent those last days of illness, personally doing the spring seeding in which his Indian helpers had prepared a few days previous. Agnes tried to persuade him to rest, and "doctored" him with sassafras tea and a dose of castor oil, but only after he had completed the spring planting did he retire to his bed. His last words were to his son, "Always be a good boy, Arthur. Mind your mother and be good to her."[14]

Death came quietly to this great man of western legend. He was laid to rest in the Genoa, Nevada Cemetery which lies at the very base of the great Sierras [sic] so well known and so often traversed by Snowshoe.[15]

Thompson's death was described in *Snowshoe Thompson*, the CVHS publication.

One day while going to the field he complained of having hot and cold spells. The next day he resorted to riding his horse to accomplish the planting and hired a neighbor boy, Robert Trimmer, to assist him. After five days of getting progressively worse

THOMPSON'S LAST YEARS

> he took to his bed and was never able to get up again. Sara Trimmer, who lived directly across the road from Thompson, helped Agnes care for him but he died on May 15, 1876. It is thought he died of appendicitis which developed into pneumonia. Services for Snowshoe were held at the Genoa Courthouse on May 19, 1876. Snowshoe claimed that from his bedroom window he could see where he picked up the quartz rock, but he died before he was able to file a claim.[16]

News of Thompson's death spread worldwide. This obituary was found in the *New York News Times,* dated May 27, 1876:

> DEATH OF SNOW-SHOE THOMPSON
> The Virginia City Enterprise
>
> A letter from our old mountain friend, Abe Rickey, informs us of the death of John A. Thompson, better known on the Pacific Coast as "Snowshoe Thompson." The man who, for twenty years, has carried the mails over the Sierras every Winter at times when the roads were blocked with snow. He died on the evening of the 15th just after a short illness.
> The old man of the mountains

John A. "Snowshoe" Thompson
Pioneer Mail Carrier of the Sierra

died as peacefully as though he had but closed his eyes to go to sleep. He caught a heavy cold about a month ago, but kept up and was able to attend to business on his ranch until about a week before his death, when his illness assumed the form of lung fever. He died at his farm in Diamond Valley, about three miles from Woodfords, Hope Valley, Alpine County, Cal. He leaves a wife and one child about 10 years of age.[17]

Headstone for John A. "Thomson"
Photo by Author

Thompson's Last Years

Some years later, after Agnes had remarried, she had a white marble headstone made with crossed skis for her departed husband, John. She had the following inscription engraved on the marker:

In Memory of
John A. Thomson [sic]
Native of Norway
Departed this life May 13, 1876
Age 49 years 10 days
Gone But not forgotten

No one knows why the letter "P" in Thompson was left out of the spelling of his last name on the headstone. Some speculate it might have been because Agnes could not read or write. When the stonemason made the error, perhaps she did not notice the misspelling.[18]

Life for Agnes had to have been difficult after John's premature death. However, she continued with the farm and enjoyed her time mothering Arthur. She must have managed the farm well, as she was able to pay the taxes. From the tax rolls:

1876, Total Taxes $107.80 Paid by A. Singleton Dec. 30, 1876.[19]

Why Agnes used her maiden name to pay these taxes will most likely never be known. By contrast, the following year she used her married name. According to the tax record it appeared that Agnes also did well the year following John's death, because her taxes increased by $388.11. The tax rolls stated:

John A. "Snowshoe" Thompson
Pioneer Mail Carrier of the Sierra

*1877, Total Taxes $488.91
Paid by Jan. 1 by Mrs. Thompson.*[20]

Just two years after the passing of her beloved John, another tragedy befell Agnes. Arthur contracted diphtheria and died on June 22, 1878.[21]

Arthur was laid to rest beside his father in the Genoa cemetery. Arthur's headstone is next to John's. Who had it made is not known. The best guess might be that Agnes ordered it and that she used the same stonemason, as both headstones have the same "Thomson" spelling.

*In Memory of
ARTHURE* [sic]
*Son & only child of
John & Agnes Thomson
Who Died June 22 1878
Age 11 Years, 4 Mos., 11 Days
Not dead but sleeping*

Headstone for Arthure *Photo by Author*

Thompson's Last Years

The following year the tax record presented a different picture. 1878-1879 Taxpayer Book.

> *Thompson, Mrs. J. A. total Taxes $48.67. Paid Dec. 20, 1878.*[22]

Could the drop in tax assessment have been caused by the tragic death of Arthur the previous spring? As a grieving widow and mother, it would be understandable if some neglect fell upon the Thompson farm.

Surprisingly, the 1879 tax book showed the tax bill more than double the preceding year, which might indicate an improvement in farming productivity.

> *Mrs. Thompson Resident of Woodfords Possession in the: W ½ of NW ¼, SE ¼ of NE ¼, Sec. 31. SW ¼ of NW ¼ Sec. 32 Township 11 Range 20E. 160 acres Total Taxes $91.98.*[23]

The increase in taxes might also have been caused by a reassessment of the Thompson's property after John's death. Then the 1880 assessment book had an interesting entry:

> *Thompson, Mrs. Agnes Resident of Woodfords Failed to give a correct statement under Description of Property. (hay added by assessor) Total Taxes $80.50.*

John A. "Snowshoe" Thompson
Pioneer Mail Carrier of the Sierra

John Scossa and Agnes Singleton Thompson Scossa
Courtesy: Douglas County Historical Society

Agnes continued her life alone for the next few years until June 10, 1884, when she married John Scossa of Carson Valley.

Thompson's Last Years

The tax record entry for the year 1884:

Agnes Thompson
Total Taxes $83.77
Paid Dec. 15 by John Scossa.
This entry was also found in the tax records:
1887 John Scossa (Married Agnes)
owner of the Thompson Ranch etc.[24]

Headstone of Agnes Scossa *Photo by Author*

Agnes's headstone is very simple. On the top edge of the headstone, it reads "Mother." It is made of black marble and the only inscription in arching letters on the front, is:

Agnes Scossa
1831-1913

John A. "Snowshoe" Thompson
Pioneer Mail Carrier of the Sierra

Agnes and John A. Thompson rest on either side of their son, Arthur, in the Genoa Cemetery.

Thompson Family Plot *Photo by Author*

11

John "Snowshoe" Thompson Remembered

Snowshoe Thompson has captured the imagination of people everywhere. There are plaques, monuments, and celebrations commemorating his exploits literally everywhere.

Those presented in this chapter are but a very few examples of these tributes. No attempt was made to find a complete list as they can be found all over the state of Nevada, the nation, and the world.

Plaques continue to be found, sometimes in the most unlikely places. The plaques, monuments, and events below are listed chronologically by date.

John A. "Snowshoe" Thompson
Pioneer Mail Carrier of the Sierra

1926 Plaque Dedication

In 2011, Steve Hale (a "Snowshoe Thompson" re-enactor) while surfing the Internet doing some research, found mention of a Thompson plaque dedicated in 1926.

It is located at Carthay Circle, a small park/traffic island, at the intersection of San Vicente and Crescent Heights, in Los Angeles, California.* This plaque, created by sculptor Henry Lion, with a relief depiction of "Snowshoe" Thompson, is attached to a granite boulder. The title of the boulder monument is "Snowshoe Thompson, or the Jedediah Strong Smith Boulder." Text from the memorial plaque:

> *A pioneer hero of the Sierras* [sic] *who for twenty winters carried the mail over the mountains to isolated camps rescuing the lost and giving succor to those in need along the way. Born 1827 Died 1876.*

This monument suggested by Miss Eudora Caroutte of Sacramento, California. Dedicated by the Native Sons of the Golden West. Assisted by the Historical Society of Southern California. Erected by the Founders of Carthay Center 1926.

---

* A photo may be found at: http://www.publicartinla.com/sculptures/pioneer.html

John "Snowshoe" Thompson Remembered

1946 Ski Club Event

A ski club held an event in Snowshoe's honor, February 23, 1946. Douglas County Ski Club sponsored a two-day ski tournament to commemorate Snowshoe Thompson. Representatives from of the Norwegian government joined the gathering Saturday morning in the Genoa cemetery for a brief ceremony to lay a wreath at Snowshoe's grave.[1]

1950 Event

An announcement of an event sponsored by the Reno Chamber of Commerce:

Welcome to Snowshoe Thompson Memorial Races.
Reno "the Biggest Little City in the World"
Welcomes You
Reno Chamber of Commerce
Convention and Tourist Bureau
5th Annual
Snowshoe Thompson
Memorial Races
White Hills Ski Area
February 25th and 26th, 1950[2]

John A. "Snowshoe" Thompson
Pioneer Mail Carrier of the Sierra

1956 Bronze Marker Placed by ECV

Another group that joined in continuing the Snowshoe Thompson mystique was a group known as E. Clampus Vitus (ECV). ECV, also known as Clampers, began as a small group of men who wanted to get together and have fun. ECV was founded by Joe Zumwalt and a group of men in 1851, in the Mother Lode mining town of Mokelumne Hill, California, about sixty miles south of the 1848 gold discovery site in Coloma, California.

The group felt the fraternal organizations of Freemasonry and the Independent Order of Odd Fellows were too serious and ritualistic.

Soon ECV fraternal chapters began springing up in nearly every mining camp. They collected funds for those injured in mining accidents and cared for widows and orphans.[3]

ECV Marker in Diamond Valley *Photo by Author*

John "Snowshoe" Thompson Remembered

Native Sons of Golden West Marker in Diamond Valley
Photo by Author

Diamond Valley with the ECV and NSGW Markers
Photo by Author

John A. "Snowshoe" Thompson
Pioneer Mail Carrier of the Sierra

The words "E. Clampus Vitus" have no apparent meaning, or Latin translation. Clampers refer to their president as the Grand Noble Humbug, with all officers having similar nonsensical titles. All members hold the same status in the organization.

There are no dues, yet they somehow seem to raise money to mark their presence by placing commemorative plaques and monuments in obscure and hard to find places.

In spite of their oft-times uncouth manner and their eagerness to act with ridiculous and raucous behavior,* they can rise to the occasion of proper decorum and do good deeds. Most of their historical marking work follows proper protocol and is historically (generally, but not always) accurate.

The Clampers founded their organization by deviating from the "acceptable and reasonable" as written by the authors in this introduction of the *History and Ritual of E. Clampus Vitus*.[4]

> *Material for this guide has been gathered from various sources including liberally plagiarizing, stealing, absconding, purloining, pilfering, looting and misappropriating the work of others. Be that as it may, I believe it is reasonably accurate. It is unsolicited, unofficial, unsanctioned, unblessed and unapproved.*

In 1956, the James Marshall Chapter #49 of ECV placed a bronze marker near Thompson's home site in Diamond Valley.

---

* Personal observation by author.

John "Snowshoe" Thompson Remembered

1957 Resolution to Commemorate Upcoming Winter Olympics Games

In 1957, a resolution was filed with the Secretary of State for the state of California. It was one of many activities to commemorate the upcoming 1960 Winter Olympic Games to be held in Squaw Valley.*

There could be a no more fitting way to commemorate and celebrate the life of Snowshoe Thompson than on an Olympics world stage.

Assembly Concurrent Resolution No. 186, Chapter 308

Assembly Concurrent Resolution No. 186—Relative to the naming of the site of the 1960 Winter Olympic Games, when included as part of the State Park System, the Snowshoe Thompson State Park.

WHEREAS, The exploits of John A. "Snowshoe" Thompson during the early years of the development of this State have made him a legendary figure in California history; and

---

* Squaw Valley is located in the Sierra Nevada, 110 miles east of Sacramento, California, 44 miles southwest of Reno, Nevada, and 8 miles from shores of Lake Tahoe.

John A. "Snowshoe" Thompson
Pioneer Mail Carrier of the Sierra

WHEREAS, "Snowshoe" Thompson gained fame through his amazing exploits in maintaining a personal mail express across the mighty Sierra Nevada Mountains [sic] *during the winter months when passage for animals and vehicles over regular roads was impossible and frequently traversed the mountains from points in the Sacramento Valley to Carson City on the eastern slope of the Sierra in less than four days; and*

WHEREAS, "Snowshoe" Thompson's mail express consisted of his personal treks over the mountains carrying the mail on his shoulders and involved physical stamina and courage of the most extraordinary kind and necessitated the personal conquest of the mightiest of mountain ranges when enveloped in the most violent of storms and blizzards; and

WHEREAS, This remarkable man employed in his trips a crude form of skis to make the perilous trips and was in all likelihood, the first person in California to use these devices which have now become so common in use for recreation in this day when man is no longer confronted with the task of combating the violence of the elements of nature for survival itself; and

John "Snowshoe" Thompson Remembered

WHEREAS, The meager records available indicate that this giant in history of the State of California received little, if any, official recognition or material reward for his fabulous exploits in behalf of the early pioneers settlers of California; and

WHEREAS, it is fitting that the memory of those who by their self-sacrifice, deed and example contributed so markedly to the development of the State and Nation be perpetuated, and because a site in the Sierra Nevada Mountains [sic], which John A. "Snowshoe" Thompson so heroically conquered in those days had been selected for the site of the 1960 Winter Olympic Games, and because it seems particularly appropriate to perpetuate the memory of one of California's outstanding historic figures by associating his name with these events; now, therefore be it

RESOLVED by the Assembly of the State of California, the Senate thereof concurring, that the site of the 1960 Winter Olympic Games, when it becomes a part of the State Park System, be named the Snowshoe Thompson State Park in Squaw Valley, California, and that action be undertaken to erect appropriate monuments to commemorate the

John A. "Snowshoe" Thompson
Pioneer Mail Carrier of the Sierra

achievement of John A. Thompson at the site; and be it further
    RESOLVED, That the Chief Clerk of the Assembly is directed to prepare suitable copies of this resolution to be sent to the State Parks Commission and Divisions of Beaches and Parks.[5]

As a point of interest, no state park has been named for Snowshoe Thompson at Squaw Valley.

1970 Induction into National Ski Hall of Fame

In 1970, Snowshoe Thompson was inducted into the National Ski Hall of Fame.[*]

The following documents show the process used to nominate him. First, a letter from the United States Ski Education Foundation:

June 2, 1970
ADDENDUM TO THE NATIONAL
SKI HALL OF FAME

The National Ski Hall of Fame Report includes a salute to Snow-

---
[*] Presently renamed the U.S. Ski and Snowboard Hall of Fame and Museum.

John "Snowshoe" Thompson Remembered

Shoe Thompson and a posthumous nomination of the California and Nevada skier for honored membership to the National Ski Hall of Fame. The committee urges that the Board of Delegates to the United State Ski Association Convention elect Snow-Shoe Thompson to the National Ski Hall of Fame, thus enabling the name John Albret* Thompson to be placed with the honored membership.

Signed by: William B. Berry, Chairman
E. O. (Buck) Erickson   Hal Laman
William McClure   T. Lee McCracken
Patricia M. Peterson   Henry J. Pflieger
Lynn H. Johnson   Vincent Rice
Edward Taylor   Enzo Serafini

Just four days later, the Sons of Norway, Snowshoe Thompson Lodge No. 78, Yuba City, California, wrote this letter:

June 6, 1970

TO WHOM IT MAY CONCERN;
By these presents, let it be known that SNOWSHOE THOMPSON LODGE NO. 78, SONS OF NORWAY, take great pride in endorsing the

---
* Teal, used the spelling Albret for Thompson's middle name.

John A. "Snowshoe" Thompson
Pioneer Mail Carrier of the Sierra

nomination of *JOHN A. (SNOWSHOE) THOMPSON* to the National Ski Hall Of Fame in Ishpeming, Michigan.

A look into history of skiing in the western part of the United States discloses that SNOWSHOE THOMPSON was among the first, if not the first, to introduce skiing to the newly developing western United States. We know of no early day pioneer who contributed more to the great winter sport of skiing, or is more worthy of the honor of being named to the United States Ski Hall Of Fame than SNOWSHOE THOMPSON.

Signed: June I. Bone* President[6]

John A. Thompson (deceased)
Year Inducted: 1970
Born: April 30, 1827 Telemark, NORWAY
Died: May 15, 1876 California

John "Snowshoe" Thompson was a legend in the mining camps of the California Sierras [sic]. With skis that were 7.5 to 8 feet long he carried the mail over the snowy mountain passes between Placerville, CA and Genoa, NV from 1856 until his death in 1876. He was a heroic figure of his day whose

---

* Was a woman president of the organization? Research reveals that "June" as a man's name was not unusual for a male, especially one of English descent.

John "Snowshoe" Thompson Remembered

efforts maintained communications throughout this remote area and demonstrated a man's capability on skis under challenging conditions

1976 Bicentennial Celebration

In January of 1976, a celebration was held in honor of the United States Bicentennial and the one hundred and twentieth year anniversary of Thompson's first mail delivery over the Sierra.[†] The event held a mail delivery re-enactment that was sponsored by the Far West Skiing Association.[‡] The chairman of the event was John Watson who wrote the following article:

BICENTENNIAL EVENT
Mail Carry
Re-enacted By John Watson

Thinking that the spirit of the Bicentennial is lost? Think that there's little interest in ski history? I can vouch

---

* Thompson's citation and his photo are displayed on the U.S. Ski Hall of Fame and Museum's website at www.skihall.com. There is a list of all the people in their Hall of Fame.
† An article in the *Reno Evening Gazette* described the course of the 1976 re-enactment of Snowshoe Thompson's historic "mail-by-ski" run.
‡ Far West Skiing Association is based in Truckee, California.

John A. "Snowshoe" Thompson
Pioneer Mail Carrier of the Sierra

that the spirit of '76 is still alive and well, that ski history lives and is celebrated in the hearts of hundreds along Snow-shoe Thompson mail route across the Sierra.

Thompson started his first winter crossing of the Sierra Nevada January 3, 1856. One hundred twenty years later, hundreds participated in the reenactment.

Thompson's crossing took three or four days, the reenactment, for logistical reasons and using modern vehicles in part, was confined to one day.

The carry started before sunrise at the very same building used as a post office in those Gold Rush days. The mail was symbolically passed to skiers on roller-skis by Lester Frost, Placerville postmaster. El Dorado County Supervisor "Budd" Lane introduced local historians and community leaders.

A car caravan led by E. Clampus Vitus carried the mail to the first over-the-snow stage at Phillips.* More than a dozen cross-country speedsters started before a greater number of "mail-carriers" and tourers, led by Royal Norwegian Consul Torvald Rafoss, departed for Echo Summit.†

The second over-the-snow stage,

---

* Town of Phillips is 45 miles east of Placerville on U.S. 50.
† Echo Summit is on U.S. 50, west of South Lake Tahoe.

John "Snowshoe" Thompson Remembered

shortened because of snow conditions, traversed the beautiful terrain around Grass Lake* with hot refreshments at Sorensen's† after the skiers and mail carriers reported in. Numbers of on lookers, historians and ski enthusiasts increased as the mail was carried farther into the snowy vastness of Hope Valley.

Meanwhile, a huge crowd was gathering in Genoa led by the Sons of Norway and local historians. Genoa's short main street was lined five deep with celebrants in this festival of American ski sport. The Carson Valley Historical Society is restoring the courthouse in this earliest Nevada settlement.

Plaques for the museum were presented Dick Goetzman and Bill Berry of the U.S. Ski Assn., Kathy Morris from the city of Placerville and Mrs. Myrtle Baker and Supervisor Thomas Stewart of El Dorado County.

Then the roller-skiers brought in the last mail pouch and presented it to John W. Warner, administrator of

---

* Grass Lake is located north of CA SR 88, off Luther Pass on CA SR 89. The summit is three miles from Hope Valley and CA SR 88 junction.
† Sorensen's Resort is located in the Carson Canyon on CA SR 88, one mile east of the junction of CA SR 88 and 89 in Hope Valley.

John A. "Snowshoe" Thompson
Pioneer Mail Carrier of the Sierra

the American Revolution Bicentennial Administration, who had flown in especially for this event, the third of the Bicentennial year.

He and Kent Williams, Bicentennial regional representative, presented special medals to the principals involved in the mail carry at a later party in Carson City.

That, briefly, was the first annual mail carry re-enactment. Many more luminaries participated than those mentioned here. The event drew enthusiasts from the farthest points of both states. If you missed it this year, don't miss it again. The mail carry has a special, convivial, historical flavor all its own.

Mrs. Jan Schlappi of the Placerville Heritage Assn. had a special insight into the man and our times.

She said, "Thompson was a loved and loving man. The people in the area admired him greatly for his physical stamina, his courage, his gentleness and his determination to bring the mail, medicines and other essentials to the remoteness of what is now western Nevada. He was truly a man for today, not just a figure of the past.[8]

John "Snowshoe" Thompson Remembered

The oldest participant to carry the mail during this re-enactment was Welie Arlen, seventy-plus years of age. These types of events are important as reminders of our rich heritage, and they will continue to keep the memory of John "Snowshoe" Thompson in the hearts and minds of adults and children everywhere.

1976 Dedication of Monument Near Donner Summit

There is an impressive monument of Snowshoe standing near the crest of the Sierra Nevada, near Donner Summit, on I-80. Located at the entrance of the Boreal Ridge Ski Resort, it is placed in front of the Western American Ski Sport Museum, which is owned and operated by the Auburn Ski Club.

This larger-than-life monument of Thompson, holding his balance pole in front of him, in a crouched position, gives the impression he is skiing down a Sierra slope at great speed. The dedication of this monument coincided with the United States Bicentennial. Following is the report of the event as it appeared in the *Sierra Sun Bonanza* on May 19, 1976.

BOREAL RIDGE
"Gone but not forgotten." These words so aptly apply to the father of

John A. "Snowshoe" Thompson
Pioneer Mail Carrier of the Sierra

American skiing and Pathfinder of the Sierra, Snow-shoe Thompson.

A 10 foot Cor•Ten steel* statue of Snow-shoe Thompson on skis with a mail pouch on his back and his ski pole in his hands on top of a 12 foot piece of granite slab that extends upward from a concrete base, was dedicated here Saturday.

Statue of Snowshoe Thompson at Boreal Ski Resort
Photo by Author

---

* A group of steel alloys which were developed to eliminate the need for painting, forming a stable rust-like appearance as if exposed to the weather for several years. *Wikipedia.*

John "Snowshoe" Thompson Remembered

"Snow-shoe was no Olympic skier or gold medal winner, but through his deeds lives on in the hearts of his countrymen and Americans," Jakob Vaage, director of the Holmenkollen Ski Museum in Oslo, Norway, told the crowd of Norwegian-Americans and ski officials and other dignitaries present at the Boreal Ridge Winter Park Saturday for the dedication of the Snow-shoe Thompson Monument. Snow-shoe, John Tostensen [Torsteinsson] was born in Telemark, Norway on April 30, 1827.

Vaage told those present for the dedication Saturday that Tostensen [Torsteinsson] *first learned about America in 1837 from two hunters who passed the farm where he and his family lived.*

It was a year later that Snow-shoe and his widowed mother emigrated to the United States. He was one of the many easterners to move west during the gold rush days. It was at this time that he assumed the name of his stepfather,* John Albret Thompson.†*Snow-shoe's fame as a skier started when he completed his first round trip between Placerville and Mormon Station, Utah Territory, a total distance of 180 miles.*

He made this trip in five days over

---

* Research has not been able to locate any conclusive information that John's mother, Gro, remarried.

† See Chapter 2.

John A. "Snowshoe" Thompson
Pioneer Mail Carrier of the Sierra

a never traveled, unmarked, mid-winter frontier route* of rugged country, with a climb and descent in each direction of the Sierras [sic]. Despite the fact he carried the mail for the U.S. Postal Service, Snow-shoe was only paid $80.37 for his 20 years of service.

Snow-shoe died at the age of 49 and is buried in the Genoa, Nevada Cemetery where his wife and son were later placed by his side.

"The dedication of Snow-shoe Thompson's statue is the highlight of your work. It is a living monument for you and Snow-shoe," a letter from the governor of Oklahoma to Angus Kent Lamar of Chikasha [Chickasha], Okla. read. Lamar was the sculptor who spent two years getting the finished work to be a close resemblance of Snow-shoe.

"He epitomized the true pioneers of our country," Rep. Harold T. "Bizz" Johnson, wrote in a letter to the Snow-shoe Thompson Lodge No. 78 of the Sons of Norway.

President Gerald Ford wrote, "History is filled with stories of remarkable men and women who did what appeared to be the impossible. The story of Snow-shoe is no legend. It is fact.

---

* Thompson was following existing wagon trails. For more information see Chapter 5.

John "Snowshoe" Thompson Remembered

He endured great hardships and personal sacrifice to fill a critical human need for communication for contact with those far away, and for news of distance places and events.

"Each person in his time," Ford wrote, "contributed in his own way."

He concluded his letter saying, "The lesson of Snow-shoe Thompson is well worth remembering in this bi-centennial year. It sets an example we must continue to follow, if we are to remain strong, vital and free."

Former Governor Ronald Reagan also sent a letter congratulating the Sons of Norway for honoring a man who exemplified the early settlers of California and who did so much for the residents of the Sierra.

Harold Moore, one of three members of the statue committee of the Snow-shoe Thompson Lodge of the Sons of Norway gave quite a tribute to Snow-shoe just prior to the unveiling of the text on the granite pillar under the statue.

Two thousand years ago a lowly carpenter,
(Jesus Christ) died.
One hundred years ago a lowly mailman
(Snow-shoe) died.

John A. "Snowshoe" Thompson
Pioneer Mail Carrier of the Sierra

*For 20 years the carpenter
labored at his task,
while the mailman also
labored at his task for 20 years.*

Moore said that while the carpenter will live on through the ages in peoples' hearts, the mailman will live on through the ages and be respected and admired. "Snow-shoe did many wonderful things as though they were ordinary things."

"There is nothing much more terrible than a winter snowstorm in the Sierra. Yet, Snow-shoe would go out into them like they were nothing out of the usual," Moore said. Wendell Robie, president of the Auburn Ski Club, reminded those present that the statue was being dedicated where visitors to California can see it.[9]

March 1976

The "Snowshoe" Thomson* Chapter No. 1827 of E. Clampus Vitus (ECV) located in Reno, Nevada,

---

* It is curious to note that these Clampers spell Snowshoe Thompson's last name without the letter P, while most everyone else spells it with the letter P. It might be speculated that the chapter chose the spelling of Thomson, which was engraved on his headstone in the Genoa cemetery.

John "Snowshoe" Thompson Remembered

(formed in 1956) laid claim to honoring the mystique of Snowshoe Thompson.

This chapter continually works hard to maintain that tradition, as seen in the chapter's use of its namesake. One of these obscure locations is at Carson Pass on CA SR 88 where they chose to place a most imposing obelisk monument resembling a miniature Washington Monument with about ten inches of the top broken off.*

In true ECV tradition, note in the following documents that the chapter obtained all the proper approvals they requested when they set about to erect this monument to honor "Snowshoe" Thompson. The idea for erecting the Snowshoe monument was given birth at an ECV chapter meeting as seen in these excerpts from their newsletter to the members.

SNOW-SHOE THOMSON
CHAPTER #1827–ECV
MARCH NEWSLETTER
76 MEETING

The regular meeting of the Chapter will be on March 9, 1976 at 8:00 PM at Charlie's Saloon and Dago String House on the corner Arlington and [illegible] streets...
Monument:
It has been proposed that

---

* The broken top was to symbolize Snowshoe's life cut short. It was adhered to the base of the monument, but has since disappeared into someone's collection. The monument's height of twenty feet represented Snowshoe's twenty years of mail delivery service.

John A. "Snowshoe" Thompson
Pioneer Mail Carrier of the Sierra

ECV Snowshoe Thompson Monument at Carson Pass
Photo by Author

John "Snowshoe" Thompson Remembered

this Chapter erect a monument to Snowshoe Thomson as stated and depicted in the Article written by Dan De Quille in the Territorial Enterprise of May 19, 1876.

The pertinent part of the article reads "There ought to be a shaft raised to Snow-shoe Thomson; not of marble; not carved and not planted in the valley, but a rough shaft of basalt or granite, massive and tall, with the top ending roughly, as if broken short, to represent a life which was strong and true to the last. And this should be upreared on the summit of the mountains over which the strong man wandered so many years, as an emblem of that life which was worn out apparently without an object."

The Chapter is looking for donations for this worthy project and is also planning to approach each of the other chapters for a donation of $100 per chapter, which will be deposited in a trust account for return in the event that sufficient funds cannot be raised. Our goal for the entire program is set at $5000. This is not an impossible amount to achieve since we have been recognition [sic] by the Nev. State Bicentennial Commission and matching funds are available.

John A. "Snowshoe" Thompson
Pioneer Mail Carrier of the Sierra

We will be contacting the Alpine County people for aid and assistance plus many hers that could contribute to this project... .The eventual location of this monument will be on either Luther Pass or Carson Pass in California... [10]

As seen by this letter on E. Clampus Vitus letterhead from John Riggs to Alpine County, the Clampers commitment was evident:

March 24, 1976
Mrs. Lucile Chain, Chairman
Alpine County Bicentennial Committee
Markleeville, CA.

Dear Mrs. Chain:

The above organization, whose territory includes Alpine County in California and Douglas County Nevada, is planning to erect a monument to Snow-shoe Thomson as narrated in Dan De Quille's article in the Territorial Enterprise of May 19, 1876. I am enclosing a copy of our chapter's newsletter in which this article is quoted. This dedication will take place sometime in July or August so as not to conflict to [sic] closely with our annual initiation in September.
We respectfully request your sanctioning of this project as a

John "Snowshoe" Thompson Remembered

ECV Carson Pass Monument Dedication Program Cover
Courtesy: Alpine County Museum

John A. "Snowshoe" Thompson
Pioneer Mail Carrier of the Sierra

Bicentennial affair and also your recognition of our Chapter as a Bicentennial organization in Alpine County. The proposed height of the monument is 20 feet, one foot for each of the 20 years that he carried the mail. It will be in granite. It is also proposed that it be erected on Carson Pass since this is one that is kept open during the winter and is generally in the center of the area that Snow-shoe Thomson traveled.

The Nevada State Bicentennial Commission has given their approval for this project along with the request that we approach the California State Bicentennial Commission to share the request for the matching funds. The cost of this project is estimated at $5000.00. We intend to raise $2500.00 of this amount and then approach the two State Commissions for their share of $1250.00 each.

Engraved invitations will be sent to all those who are of special interest in this project who are not Clampers.

Clampers will receive a special proclamation. As you can see by the news letter we will be having a steak feed and bar set up at the site for everyone to partake off [sic]. *There will be no initiation. If you would like for me to come to one of your meetings to explain this further, please feel free*

John "Snowshoe" Thompson Remembered

> to contact me at the address or phone number listed below.
> "Satisfactory"
> John W. Riggs, Sr. XNGH
> Monument Committee Chairman
> Reno, NV[11]

It did not take long for John Riggs to receive a response from Alpine County.

> Markleeville, Calif.
> April 8, 1976
> John W. Riggs, Sr.,
> Monument Committee Chr.
> Reno, Nev.
>
> Dear Mr. Riggs,
>
> Your letter of March 24, to Mrs. Chain was received and read and considered with considerable interest at our Board of Directors meeting last evening. For you information the Board of the Historical Society was appointed by the Board of Supervisors to act as the Bi-Centennial Committee.
> Our interest in your proposed monument was sincere, due to the fact that we have a special interest in Snowshoe Thompson. His home was

John A. "Snowshoe" Thompson
Pioneer Mail Carrier of the Sierra

in Diamond Valley, we have in our museum his citizenship document, a handmade chair of his, newspaper clippings, etc. Not only that, but we feel that we have a site on Carson Pass, which would be most appropriate for the monument. It is historically significant due to the fact that the cache he used for his skis and his supplies is within walking distance of the highway.*

Consequently, serving two capacities as Historical and Bi-Centennial we offer our endorsement of your project as well as our support in any way we can. I am sure our local members of the Clampers will join in this support.

We would like to suggest, if possible that you arrange to make a visit to the Alpine County to look over the site we propose as well as discuss in what way we can be helpful.

As long as Mr. Love and I live at Woodfords, arrangements can be made to meet here with board members from Markleeville. You have been to our home before, when you came to

---

* It is neither clear, nor known at this time, where that location might have been, unless she is referring to the "Snowshoe Thompson Cave," which is located about eighteen miles east of Carson Pass and would be within walking distance of the highway.

John "Snowshoe" Thompson Remembered

see Judge Love (now retired). We live in the same place.

We hope to hear from you soon.

Sincerely,
Mabel C. Love (signature)
Secretary

1977 Dedication Ceremony

July 10, 1977, the Nevada Clampers held a dedication ceremony for this monument and it was obvious to those attending that the Clampers had worked hard and spent a lot of money. However, they could not resist falling back to their basic outrageous behavior as observed in this handout with a well illustrated cover.

Page 2 of the program pictured a nice portrait of Snowshoe and a full-page biography, with only a few errors in the text. Page 3 quoted an article from the *Territorial Enterprise* that was a repeat of the article quoted from the ECV newsletter of March 24, 1976. The back cover had the agenda for the day's event, and was followed by this clever poem:

John A. "Snowshoe" Thompson
Pioneer Mail Carrier of the Sierra

"Quicksilver" beat old "Snowshoe" bad,
In days of Sixty-nine
La Porte was thrilled with voices glad
Along their steep incline.

Came "Snowshoe" home a-feeling low
To Alpine County high
Great Silver Mountain felt the blow
Where regions pierce the sky.

The price of Noble whisky fell
No miner drank a drop
Till Plumas County went to hell
And Alpine stood on top.

"Snowshoe" smeared not his skis with dope
Alas, fate let him down
Miners, with souls full of hope
Raised money 'round the Town

"Come on you blanket Plumas guys–
Alturas snowshoe men"
But no one came to win the prize
All stayed within their den.

Skyhawk[*][12]

---

[*] W. F. Skyhawk was Hubert Hamlin's pen name. He was editor of the Knott Reminisces.

John "Snowshoe" Thompson Remembered

1986 Marker placed at Genoa Courthouse Museum

The ECV Snowshoe Thomson Chapter #1827 placed a granite marker with a bronze plaque in front of the Genoa Courthouse Museum in Genoa. This beautiful plaque commemorates Snowshoe Thompson and celebrates their thirtieth-year anniversary of their Clamper charter.

This beautiful plaque does contain some errors, such as the misspelling of his birth name and use of the word "Sierras." However, it should be noted that on the plaque they spelled Thompson's last name with the letter P; not only that, they used the letter P in their chapter name.

The last few lines of the plaque read:

The Bravest are the Tenderest
Dedicated in Genoa Nevada,
September 6, 1986
On this 30th Anniversary of
"Snowshoe" Thompson Chapter No. 1827
E. Clampus Vitus
5961-5991

The numbers at the bottom appear to be some type of obscure code placed to baffle the reader and be consistent with the Clamper's warped sense of humor.

John A. "Snowshoe" Thompson
Pioneer Mail Carrier of the Sierra

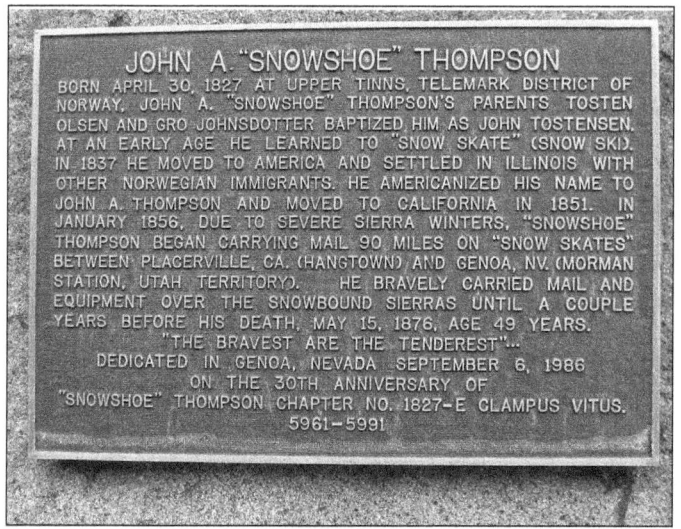

ECV Snowshoe Thompson Plaque at Genoa Museum
Photo by Author

According to one Clamper, if you subtract the first number from the second number, you come up with 30, which is the anniversary of the chapter formation. If you subtract 4005 (4005 represents 4005 B.C. that some Clampers claim is the original date of the founding of ECV), from 5991, you come up with 1986. Therefore, to be consistent in their fun-loving mischievous behavior, they continue to try to mess with our minds.

1988 Resolution for
Snowshoe Thompson Day

John "Snowshoe" Thompson Remembered

This next resolution came from the governor of Nevada, dated April 20, 1988:

WHEREAS, "Snowshoe" Thompson, a brave and fearless mountaineer, was the human link between the eastern and western slopes of the Sierra Nevada carrying mail and supplies to the people in Genoa and neighboring communities for almost 20 years; and

WHEREAS, "Snowshoe" Thompson born in Norway on April 30, 1827, fashioned the first pair of Norwegian snowshoes ever seen in the Sierra, and 1 January, 1856 glided over 30 to 50 feet deep snow to make his first mail run from Placerville to Carson Valley, a distance of 90 miles; and

WHEREAS, "Snowshoe" Thompson had no fear of the fierce winters, "the storms that rocked the pine but did not stir his Norwegian blood—the blood of the old Vikings—and aroused in him a spirit of defiance, a desire to sally forth and battle with the genii and the tempest;" and

WHEREAS, "Snowshoe" Thompson

John A. "Snowshoe" Thompson
Pioneer Mail Carrier of the Sierra

travelled day and night, usually on time, and was guided by the pines and rock formation by day, and by the stars at night; and

WHEREAS, "Snowshoe" Thompson not only brought newspapers from other parts of the country to Nevada, but carried much of the material on which the "Territorial Enterprise" was printed, a weekly publication first printed in Genoa on December 18, 1858; and

WHEREAS, "Snowshoe" Thompson's final resting place is in Genoa, next to his son, Arthur, "at home where the snowy peaks of his loved mountains looked down upon his last camping place; where voices of the pines are born to him by every breeze;" and

WHEREAS, in recognition and appreciation of "Snowshoe" Thompson's many exemplary contributions to the silver state and in celebration of Nevada's legendary mail carrier's birthday, the town of Genoa, in conjunction with the United States Postal Service, is holding a day of celebration in his honor;

John "Snowshoe" Thompson Remembered

NOW, THEREFORE, I, Richard H. Bryn, governor of the state of Nevada, do hereby proclaim April 30, 1988 as "Snowshoe Thompson Day" in Nevada and call on all citizens to join in this special tribute.

IN WITNESS WHEREOF, I have hereunto set my hand and caused the great Seal of the State of Nevada to be affixed at the State Capitol in Carson City, this 20th day of April, in the year of Our Lord one thousand nine hundred and eighty-eight.[13]

1988 Snowshoe Thompson Day Celebration

The invitation to another interesting event that was held in Placerville in 1988, read:
*You are cordially invited to attend the
Snowshoe Thompson Day Celebration
Honoring the
County's Pioneer Trans – Sierra Mail Carrier
10:00 A.M. Saturday April 30, 1988
at The Placerville Post Office
for The First Presentation of the U.S. Postal Service*

John A. "Snowshoe" Thompson
Pioneer Mail Carrier of the Sierra

*Snowshoe Thompson Award of Honor
to be presented by Arthur I. Montoya
General Manager/Postmaster,
Sacramento Division, and
First Issuance of the official
Snowshoe Thompson Cachet Envelopes
By The Heritage Association of El Dorado County
This Observance of Snowshoe Thompson
Day to be held under the auspices of
The Heritage Association of El Dorado County
and The U.S. Postal Service,
Sacramento Division* [14]

1990 Plaque Dedication

Thompson's Diamond Valley homestead is the site of another plaque honoring Snowshoe.

*SNOWSHOE THOMPSON HOME
John A. "Snowshoe" Thompson
(1827 – 1876)
Native of Norway who carried the
mail across the Sierra Nevada on Skis,
assisting the needful for twenty years,
dwelt and died on this site.
Dedicated June 30, 1990
Native Sons of the Golden West
Joseph L. Neitzel, Grand President
Fund by James D. Phelan Trust**

---
* See photo on page 200

John "Snowshoe" Thompson Remembered

1999 Snowshoe Thompson Cross Country Ski Snowshoe Tour Established

One of the more active local organizations in Genoa, dedicated to preserving "Snowshoe" Thompson's memory and keeping his spirit alive and well, is the "Friends of Snowshoe Thompson."

Nina Eggen MacLeod initiated the first Snowshoe Thompson Cross Country Ski Snowshoe Tour in 1999.

This tour event continues to be celebrated annually on the first Saturday in March to commemorate Snowshoe's life and is held in the setting traversed by Thompson for twenty-plus winters and numerous times in the summertime in Hope Valley.* It is in the general location where Thompson and the Sisson rescue party spent that night in the blizzard of December 1856.†

In March 1999, only about six people attended; in 2000, about ten to twenty people; in 2001, about eight people, but there was no snow; in 2002, about ten people showed up. The number of attendees would grow and wane as the weather and snow varied.

---

* Hope Valley, California, is twenty-five miles south of the South Lake Tahoe, California.
† See Chapter 5.

John A. "Snowshoe" Thompson
Pioneer Mail Carrier of the Sierra

2000 Snowshoe Thompson Committee Established

The group began as the Snowshoe Thompson Committee of The Greater Genoa Business Association, Genoa, Nevada. The committee joined with Nina Eggen MacLeod in 2000 after her first Snowshoe Thompson Cross Country Ski Snowshoe Tour was held in 1999. The committee set about to raise funds to commission a bronze statue of Snowshoe to be placed at the Mormon Station State Park in Genoa, Nevada. This was the announcement of their fundraising goal for this monument.

*A Monumental Tribute
to Snowshoe Thompson
Brick by Brick*

Members of the Greater Genoa Business Association have undertaken the project to erect a statue to honor a great Norwegian-American, John "Snowshoe" Thompson, in the center of Genoa in the Mormon Station State Park. A brick wall will surround a life-size bronze sculpture on "Snowshoe," created by Colorado sculptor, Don Budy.* You can become part of the

---

* Visit *www.BronzesByBudy.com*, the artist's website, to see a photo of his Thompson statue

John "Snowshoe" Thompson Remembered

history of Genoa by having your name or the name of loved ones, grandchildren, groups, or organizations engraved on a brick for a tax-deductible minimum donation of $100 per brick.*

John "Snowshoe" Thompson delivered mail and other goods, including medicines, over a treacherous 90-mile route through the Sierra from Genoa to Placerville.

He made this trip twice a month every winter from 1856 to 1876. His treks were made on what was probably the first pair of wooden skis in the West. He was never fully compensated by the Postal Service for his efforts and dangerous ventures. "Snowshoe" is buried in the Genoa Cemetery.

You can help us build a tribute to this heroic man. The project is being financed entirely by donation. Our goal is $50,000; we have reached $30,000 to date. To make a donation and/or learn more about the "Snowshoe" Thompson memorial project please contact: Sue Knight or Greater Genoa Business Association, Genoa, NV. [15]

The 2000 officers of the Snowshoe Thompson Committee of The Greater Genoa Business Association were:

---

* The author and his wife were proud contributors and still experience a thrill when seeing "our brick" in the base of the monument.

John A. "Snowshoe" Thompson
Pioneer Mail Carrier of the Sierra

President, Les Kynett
Committee Chairperson, Bill Bowersock
Secretary, Sue Knight

Statue of Snowshoe Thompson at Mormon Station
Photo by Author

John "Snowshoe" Thompson Remembered

Plaque at Statue of Snowshoe Thompson
Photo by Author

2001 Statue Unveiled

On June 23, 2001, a dedication and celebration was held with the unveiling of the statue placed in the center of Genoa in the Mormon Station State Park.

Thirty of Snowshoe's relatives and their friends from his birthplace in Norway, in addition to many people from the United States, attended this momentous occasion.

2001 Snowshoe's Route Retraced

John A. "Snowshoe" Thompson
Pioneer Mail Carrier of the Sierra

In 2001, three young men from Reno, Nevada, retraced Snowshoe's route from Placerville to Genoa, using high tech equipment, wearing Gortex clothing, and eating dried (reconstituted) food. It took them six days. (Note: it took Snowshoe five days for round trip). As they limped into Genoa with blisters on their feet, they expressed their admiration for the legendary Snowshoe Thompson.[16]

2003 Friends of Snowshoe Thompson Becomes a Non-profit Organization

On October 6, 2003, "Friends of Snowshoe Thompson" officially became a non-profit organization. It is composed of a rather casual, though hard working, group of people who take very seriously their commitment to keep the memory of this great man alive.

> *The purpose of the organization is:*
> *To promote and foster the memory of John "Snowshoe" Thompson through events and activities, and to maintain the statue and planter in Mormon Station State Park.*

> *The mission is:*
> *To honor his memory in many ways, including promotion of international cooperation between Norwegian and*

John "Snowshoe" Thompson Remembered

American communities; promotion of connection between American Lutheran Churches and Scandinavian Lutheran Churches, encouraging education in the schools about Norwegians in America; and holding events supporting these ideas.[17]

Friends of Snowshoe Thompson has minimal dues and is mighty in spirit when raising money to maintain monuments, to hold events honoring "Snowshoe," and presenting programs about the history of the area during his lifetime. 2012 Friends officers were: President Bill Bowersock, Secretary Sue Knight, and Treasurer Loraine Dix. Directors: Ted Tiffany, liaison with the Carson Valley Historical Society; Nina MacLeod, liaison between Genoa, Nevada, and Norway; Kerstin Wolle, Steve Hale, and Honorary Friends Member, sculptor Don Budy.

2004 Friends of Snowshoe Thompson Activities

The first official Friends activity of 2004 was to continue the annual Snowshoe Thompson Cross Country Ski Snowshoe Tour gatherings in Hope Valley. Profits from the annual event support the maintenance of the statue and presentations to

John A. "Snowshoe" Thompson
Pioneer Mail Carrier of the Sierra

educate children and members of the organization to continue the legacy of "Snowshoe" and the history of the surrounding area.

True to the "Friends of Snowshoe Thompson" mission statement, they hosted an event on September 18, 2004, to honor their Lutheran Church commitment. The Friends joined with the Evangelical Lutheran Church in America and the Lutheran Churches of Scandinavia as the church representatives dedicated a plaque. The celebration program read:

Welcome and Hymn,
Pastor Ross F. Hidy, President
Lutheran History Center of the West

Greeting and Devotions,
Pastor Scott Minke, Dean of the Sierra Conference,
Sierra Pacific Synod

Introductions of Special Guests:
The Genoa Cemetery Committee
President Wallace Adams
Friends of Snowshoe Thompson
President Bill Bowersox *
Carson Valley Historical Society
Mary Ellen Conaway,
Director of Museums
Nevada State Parks David Morrow,
Administrator
The Town of Genoa
Paul Williams, Town Manager
Message and Dedication of the Plaque

* The correct spelling is Bowersock.

John "Snowshoe" Thompson Remembered

Rev. David Mullen, Bishop of the Sierra Pacific Synod, For the 65 Synods of the Evangelical Lutheran Church in America and The Lutheran Churches of Scandinavia
Closing Word of Appreciation and Thanks
Hymn of Joy Lord's Prayer and Benediction
The following brief narrative was included:

Three Churches were important to John Thompson. Atraa Lutheran Church, where Jon Torsteinson [Torsteinsson]-Rue was baptized on May 24, 1827 was a wooden Stave Church* that had been built in 1180. That parish was divided in 1888 and a new building erected. But in 1837 Jon left for America with his Mother. They lived in various places, but apparently after his Mother died, John moved to Wisconsin to join his brother, Tosten [sic] and they all worshiped in historic Old Muskego Church. But there was much sickness in that swampy area that most families moved to higher ground near Mt. Horeb. There they worshiped in Springdale Lutheran Church. The California Gold Rush led many to the Sierras [sic] and John headed West to try his luck. Later John became famous for carrying mail on his snowshoes over the Sierras [sic]. This Viking Norwegian we honor today

---

*A photo of the Stave church is on page 2

John A. "Snowshoe" Thompson
Pioneer Mail Carrier of the Sierra

became a legend.

History is a jig-saw puzzle. Today new pieces give us a greater understanding of the life of pioneers like Snowshoe.* The Carson Valley is blessed with people who honor their pioneers and preserve history. Today people love to visit their superb Museums and State Parks. Excellent staff and very dedicated volunteers keep their programs and displays in top condition. No wonder visitors love to come to the Carson Valley and learn of the history of the West.[18]

Plaque in front of the headstone at Thompson's grave
Photo by Author

---

* This quote is the opening citation in this book.

John "Snowshoe" Thompson Remembered

The plaque reads:
WE SALUTE
JOHN "SNOWSHOE" THOMPSON

On his homemade Snowshoes John carried the mail and supplies over the snowy Sierras [sic] for 20 winters. As he traveled he saved the lives of seven people who were snowbound in mountains cabins. In 1866, after this tall Norwegian became an American citizen, he homesteaded a 160 acre ranch in Diamond Valley. Respected by all who knew him, John was elected to the Alpine County Board of Supervisors.

A TRIBUTE
FROM THREE LUTHERAN CHURCHES

Atraa Lutheran Church in Telemark, Norway...where John was baptised and the two Wisconsin churches where John worshipped with his family: Historic Old Muskego Lutheran Church and Springdale Lutheran Church in Mt. Horeb. Then Snowshoe joined the rush to California. Though he found no gold, Snowshoe Thompson became famous as the "mailman" of the Sierras [sic] who brought skiing to the West."
   From Fellow Lutherans of America and Scandinavia[*] [19]

---

[*] An interesting observation is that there is no date on this plaque.

John A. "Snowshoe" Thompson
Pioneer Mail Carrier of the Sierra

Rue family farm in Norway
Courtesy: Nina Eggers MacLeod

John "Snowshoe" Thompson Remembered

2006 Ski Event in Norway

In 2006, the twentieth anniversary of a twenty-kilometer ski event took place in Tinn, Norway, commemorating the life of Snowshoe Thompson. Some six hundred people participated in that event.*

There are many Snowshoe markers in Norway celebrating Jon Torsteinsson Rue's life. One such site is shown on the dedication page of this book.

2009 Anniversary Celebration

"Friends of Snowshoe Thompson" decided to host a "Snowshoe Thompson" celebration every five years at Mormon Station in Genoa, Nevada, in the park to commemorate the dedication of the statue of Snowshoe.

Here is the announcement:

> "Friends of Snowshoe Thompson"
> *Snowshoe Thompson*
> *Celebrating the 10th Anniversary*
> *of the Snowshoe Thompson Statue*
> *Dedication*
> *Sunday, June 19th – 2 p.m.*

---

* Nina Eggers MacLeod shared her experiences via email with the author after she attended the event in Norway.

John A. "Snowshoe" Thompson
Pioneer Mail Carrier of the Sierra

*Entertainment, refreshments,
FREE admission
to the new
Snowshoe Thompson exhibit
in the
Genoa Courthouse Museum
followed by
a concert
Genoa Town Park
with MONIQUE
and
the KINGTONES.*

Bring a picnic, beverage and a lawn chair!

2011 Sculpture Erected in Squaw Valley

Remember that resolution from the State of California stating that the site of the 1960 Winter Olympics Games at Squaw Valley was to become a state park, named after Snowshoe—and nothing ever came of it? Well, since then the Squaw Valley ski area has been developed into a mega ski resort with private homes, condominiums, restaurants, an upscale shopping mall, and a golf course, which fill the valley.

However, not everyone forgot about the resolution to commemorate Snowshoe Thompson at Squaw Valley. In 2011, the Sons of Norway Lodge,

John "Snowshoe" Thompson Remembered

6-078, of Yuba City, California, erected a metal sculpture of Snowshoe Thompson at the west end of the walking mall in Squaw Valley resort. This monument depicts a standing Thompson, holding his skis upright, gazing up at the mountain where thousands of skiers today enjoy the sport that he helped popularize some 140 years ago.

These younger, modern-day skiers use high tech equipment* and scientifically formulated ski wax† to enjoy the thrill of the sport. Most of them probably have no awareness of how the sport began or of the founders of old. This monument has high exposure to hundreds, if not thousands, of people who walk past it daily. Many stop to read the plaque and to have their picture taken with it, such as this author.

2011 Annual Tour

In 2011, the Friends continued the tradition with the Twelfth Annual Snowshoe Thompson Cross Country Ski Snowshoe Tour celebration for well over seventy-five people who attended under cold, but sunny skies.

---

* See 2001 reenactment of Snowshoe's route, as submitted by Sue Knight, is earlier in this chapter.
† La Porte boys ski wax – dope - is explained in Chapter 8.

John A. "Snowshoe" Thompson
Pioneer Mail Carrier of the Sierra

Author with Statue of Snowshoe Thompson at Squaw Valley Ski Resort

John "Snowshoe" Thompson Remembered

2012 Thirteenth Annual Snowshoe Tour Celebration

The Thirteenth Annual Snowshoe Thompson Cross Country Ski Snowshoe Tour celebration was held March 3, 2012, and was quite different from other years, in regard to weather, snow, and attendance. In the winter of 2011-2012, the snow had been light, sporadic, and spotty in the Sierra, as it was in all of northern California. In fact, February 28, four days before the celebration, the Hope Valley location was mostly mud.

On February 29 and March 1 a light, two-day snowstorm covered the warm ground with just enough snow to cover rocks and tree branches, which allowed the twenty-five or more people attending to follow "Snowshoe" by snowshoeing (on traditional snowshoes, not skis) up the groomed trail.

Traditional activities that highlight this celebration include an opportunity to cross-country ski or snowshoe with Nina Macleod,* the leader since 1999, and learn some Norwegian history.

Steve Hale, a retired U.S. Forest Service employee, also entertained participants by

---
* MacLeod was born in Norway and has lived in the South Lake Tahoe area most of her life. She has been instrumental in organizing numerous Snowshoe Thompson celebrations. She has also been the driving influence in this author's decision to write this book.

John A. "Snowshoe" Thompson
Pioneer Mail Carrier of the Sierra

convincingly portraying "Snowshoe" and leading one of the snowshoe groups.

This author has been honored to speak on Snowshoe Thompson, along with other lecturers, at each event since 1999. In the afternoon, folks attending were offered an opportunity to try skiing on "Long Boards."*

The list of activities sometimes varies depending on the weather; however, fiddle music, food, and drinks are always part of the celebration.

Snowshoe Thompson Ski-Snowshoe Tour in Hope Valley
Photo by Author

---

* See Chapter 8.

John "Snowshoe" Thompson Remembered

Other

Numerous organizations, clubs, and associations continue to celebrate and honor Snowshoe Thompson and his Sierra experiences.

To find those who have recognized Snowshoe Thompson with resolutions, celebrations, and monuments, one only needs to keep an eye out, no matter the city, state, or county.

Presented in this chapter is only a small sampling of just how much Thompson was loved and remembered.

John A. "Snowshoe" Thompson
Pioneer Mail Carrier of the Sierra

SNOWSHOE THOMSON

Scion of mighty Vikings;
Master of the drifted snow;
With only the stars to guide you
And the instincts of where to go,
On, On you pressed toward summits,
On, On with the precious mail,
Climbing, yes, ever upward
Over the blinded trail.

The whistling blizzards fought you,
And the teeth of the biting cold,
But you faltered not, John Thomson,
For the will, inside, was bold.
From Hangtown on to Carson
Your hand hewn skis have gone,
The ancient pines that whisper
Tell, often, what you've done.

Strawberry's cave still echoes,
And the Lover's Leap resounds,
Strange voices in the offing-
As, by night, your swift ghost bound;
Genoa breathes your spirit;
Up where the blizzards rage
There's a voice in the high Sierra
That sings to Nevada's sage.

Poem by Skyhawk[20]

John A. "Snowshoe" Thompson
Pioneer Mail Carrier of the Sierra

Appendix

A	Carson Pass
B	Thomas Knott
C	Placerville
D	Yolo County
E	Crossing the Isthmus of Panama
F	Pony Express
G	Daggett Pass
H	Roger's Cabin
I	W. F. Skyhawk
J	Augustus T. Dowd
K	Konigsberg
L	Post Office History

APPENDIX

A
Carson Pass

This route was opened in 1848 (Consider reading *Gold Rush Trail* by Frank Tortorich for this history) and became the main gold rush route until 1852, when the Johnson Cutoff and other routes were opened. The Carson River Route terminated in Placerville, as did the Johnson Cutoff.

B
Thomas Knott

April 13, 1808 – February 16, 1887

The *Knott Reminiscences* is a document that has been overlooked by many people doing research on Snowshoe Thompson. This eyewitness account is consistent with other early day descriptions of the beginnings of the Utah Territory (Nevada) areas of Carson Valley, Genoa, and Eagle Valley (Carson City). Knott introduces facts that Thompson was carrying the mail over the Sierra in the winter between Placerville and Genoa, and was working in these areas as early as 1853, three years before De Quille dates Thompson first carrying mail in the winter of 1856. Other writers used De Quille's date. Knott fills in the blank period of Thompson's life between his failed gold mining efforts in 1851 and his working on the ranch near Putah Creek in the Sacramento Valley in 1857.

John A. "Snowshoe" Thompson
Pioneer Mail Carrier of the Sierra

When John Thompson was mining in Coon Hollow and Kelsey, he met Thomas Knott and his son Elzy, who came to Placerville in 1852 and worked in a hardware store. Most likely every miner in the area would have gone to that hardware store for supplies and mining equipment.

The Knotts came to California by way of the Carson River Route, just as John Thompson did a year earlier. All three of these men passed through Carson Valley and most probably stopped at Mormon Station.

Thomas Knott hired Thompson to go back over the Sierra to Carson Valley and help build sawmills. Knott was a skilled and experienced millwright and had built a number of mills in the Midwest. He tells of having Thompson carry his personal mail west over the mountains in the winter of 1853-54 on Norwegian snow-skates.

Knott's journals of those early days are signed and dated, January 28, 1881. It is acknowledged that facts can become clouded with time and most certainly age. However, Knott's writings seem consistent with other research available and are backed by Thomas Knott's son, Albert, and what is referred to as the testimony of Thomas Knott's granddaughter, Elyzett Knott Selby.

Herbert Hamlin interviewed Albert Knott at the spry age of ninety-eight and interviewed Elyzett Knott Selby, the only child by Knott's son Elzy, in circa 1941. She was born in 1859, grew up in Genoa, Nevada, and died at the age of eighty-five in 1944.

Herbert Hamlin was the editor of *Pony Express Courier* and became fascinated with the Thompson story after running across the Knott journal. He

APPENDIX

traveled the distance of 185 miles on today's U.S. 50, between Genoa and Austin, talking to old timers and seeking out documents of those early days. Having lived in Utah at one time, Hamlin was able to obtain the Mormon perspective.

When Hamlin first connected with Elyzett in Genoa, she was standoffish and hesitant to talk with him. She said to him "What do you want here—the real story of this town, or the Mormon history?" It is important to know that Elyzett's father, Elzy, was killed by a Mormon man seven months before her birth in 1859. Hamlin assured Elyzett that he was after the real history; she then relaxed and openly shared her memories.

Not much is written about Thomas Knott. Bancroft's *History of Nevada* gives Knott only a few lines in the footnotes regarding early settlers. When Hamlin edited the *Knott Reminiscences*, published circa 1947 by the *Mountain Democrat* in Placerville, California, he divided the *Knott Reminiscence* into six parts.

1. Introduction of Albert Knott.
2. Introduction to the Knott reminiscences and some background history of early Nevada. The Thomas Knott journal.
3. Hamlin's edit of the Knott Journal.
4. Reminiscences of Albert Knott.
5. Testimony by Elyzett Knott Selby from her interview by Herbert Hamlin.
6. "Brigham And His Early-Day Retinue Of Bowers," a one-page story of the Mormon occupation in Genoa and the area.

John A. "Snowshoe" Thompson
Pioneer Mail Carrier of the Sierra

Hamlin must have taken it upon himself to use Thompson's name without the letter P throughout his *Knott Reminiscences* work, most likely taking the spelling of Thomson from Snowshoe's headstone in the Genoa Cemetery. In his journal, Thomas Knott never used any name for John "Snowshoe" Thompson, but referred to him as "the Norwegian."

The great importance of Hamlin's work (*Knott Reminiscences: Early History of Nevada in the 1850s*. Edited by H. Hamlin) is best described in the foreword by Dr. Charles L. Camp, a paleontologist, University of California, a Western Historian, and editor of many pioneer journals and diaries:

> *Mr. Herbert Hamlin has done a distinct service to the Western history in collecting and publishing the records of the pioneers. Much original material has already appeared in Mr. Hamlin's* Pony Express Courier *and these reminiscences of the Nevada pioneer Thomas Knott, are especially important and unusual, detailing little known incidents of the life at the rugged outpost of Genoa on the eastern slope of the Sierra.*
>
> *Thomas Knott, like James Marshall, was a millwright who knew how to make a saw mill, a grist mill or a wagon wheel, with only the most primitive tools and materials. He built many mills and not the least of these was the one at Mormon Station (Genoa). Here he lost his son in a Mormon fight, but he held out against*

Appendix

great odds when his mill products became vitally necessary to the support of the emigrants at the Washoe Mines.

His own story and the recollections of his family are here gathered together to illuminate a peculiar phase of the Western struggler for existence, when, in the fifties, Mormon and gentile clashed on the far eastern borders of California.

Charles L. Camp
University of California
February 7, 1947

Thomas Knott related numerous activities that took place in the Carson Valley in the early 1850s. He built sawmills at Woodfords, Genoa, and Eagle Valley, selling out with little profit. Knott was involved building toll roads at Woodfords Station on the Carson River Route. With iron being difficult to obtain, Knott went along the emigrant trail collecting iron discarded along the route from abandoned wagons to fabricate items for his mill building endeavors.

Knott reminisced of many of the early settlers in the Carson Valley. He and his son Elzy faced numerous problems with the Mormon settlers, as did many other "gentile" settlers in the Carson Valley. He related events involving the Pony Express, the Pyramid Lake War, and the building of Fort Churchill on the Carson River. Knott was friends with both Washoe and Paiute tribes, knew Chief Winnemucca, and befriended Kit Carson when he traveled through Carson Valley in 1853.

All historians, professional and arm chair alike,

John A. "Snowshoe" Thompson
Pioneer Mail Carrier of the Sierra

reading these *Knott Reminiscences* can appreciate the wealth of information they contain, especially for this author, who was able to fill in some pieces of the puzzle when writing this study.

C
Placerville

The progression of the names for Placerville's names: "Old Dry Digging" after gold was discovered in 1848 in nearby Coloma; followed by "Hangtown" in 1849 when hangings were used as a means of crime deterrent, and after years of prodding—mainly by the town's women—in 1854, the "City of Placerville" was incorporated.

D
Yolo County

This county has retained excellent records of all land deeds, purchases, and sales since before California's statehood in 1850. It is also one of the original counties and, to date, it has never changed its shape or size.

E
Crossing the Isthmus of Panama

The Chagres River was navigable by small boats to within ten to fifteen miles of the Pacific Ocean. Therefore, the mail (and steamship passengers)

Appendix

had to be transported overland to the Pacific Ocean. Ships would pick up the mail in Panama City. In 1855, a trans-panama railroad was completed, making the trip across the isthmus safer and faster. The Panama Canal was not completed until 1914.

F
Pony Express

The Pony Express trail ran from St. Joseph, Missouri, to Sacramento, California, and was 1,840 miles in length. Upon arrival in Sacramento, the mail was placed on a steamer and continued down the Sacramento River to San Francisco for a total of 1966 miles. The Pony Express Trail went through the present states of Missouri, Kansas, Nebraska, Wyoming, Colorado, Utah, Nevada, and California.

G
Daggett Pass

Daggett Pass Trail, named for C. D. Daggett, who acquired land at its foot in 1854, was earlier called Georgetown Pack Trail. Replaced in 1860 by a wagon road built by Kingsbury and McDonald, for which they received a territorial franchise in 1881, it shortened the distance between Sacramento and Virginia City by 15 miles.

The road cost $585,000 toll receipts were $190,000 in 1863. Heavy eastward travel occurred 1860 to 1868. The toll for a wagon and four horses was

John A. "Snowshoe" Thompson
Pioneer Mail Carrier of the Sierra

$17.50. Round trip from Shingle Springs, California, to Henry Van Sickle's Station near the foot of the range. Van Sickle, who helped finance the road, eventually acquired it and sold it to Douglas County in 1889 for $1000. Ironic.

Horse-drawn water carts sprinkled summer dust, and sleds packed winter snow providing a year-round hard surfaced road.

Pony Express and the line of the Humboldt & Salt Lake Telegraph Company followed Kingsbury Grade. Nevada Historic Marker # 117 spells Daggett with one T.

H
Roger's Cabin

The "Uncle Billy" Rogers cabin was located near Red Lake, where he had a copper mine. Thompson was following the Carson River Route going over Carson Pass. This route was opened in 1848 (Consider reading *Gold Rush Trail*, Tortorich, for this history) and became the main gold rush route until 1852, when the Johnson Cutoff and other routes were opened.

I
W. F. Skyhawk

W. F. Skyhawk, the *nom de plume* of one Herbert Hamlin. He wrote poems, such as *Down Genoa's Peak Descending* and was the author of a

APPENDIX

series of articles beginning in the June 1941 issue of the *Pony Express Courier* on the life and times of Snowshoe Thompson. The articles ran until February 1941 and were reprinted in the late 1940s in the same journal.

Hamlin was captivated by the exploits of Snowshoe Thompson and he quoted an unknown author who "considered him to be a 'Hero without parallel' who could fly down the Sierras on his skis at a speed of eighty feet per second." (John A. Snowshoe Thompson Collection, Alpine County. Museum, Markleeville, CA.)

J
Augustus T. Dowd

Dowd is credited as having discovered a grove of giant sequoias (redwood trees). He was not the first one to see the trees, but it was in his sharing of this discovery that led to the popularity of an area now known as Calaveras Big Trees State Park, located four miles northeast of Arnold, California, on CA SR 4.

K
Konigsberg

Identified by many names before the town was called Silver Mountain City, it was known as Kongsberg, per *Early Towns and Villages in Alpine County, 1943*, per U.S. Geographic Names information Service (GNIS.gov). In Norway, there

John A. "Snowshoe" Thompson
Pioneer Mail Carrier of the Sierra

was a town originally named Konigs Bierg with a modern day name of Kongsberg. Founded in 1624, it was home to intensive silver mining from 1623–1957.

Königsberg was a town in East Prussia founded in 1255 where silver was mined. (*Wikipedia*)

Both names mean King Mountain to honor reigning kings. Silver Mountain City, elevation of 6,411 feet, is five miles north-northeast of Ebbetts Pass. Additional information on Silver Mountain City can be found in David L. Durham's book, *California's Geographic Names: A Gazetteer of Historic and Modern Names of the State* (Clovis, CA: Quill Driver Books, 1998).

The author chose to use the spelling Konigsberg based on Karen Dustman's carefully researched book on Silver Mountain City.

L
Post Office History

The U.S. Postal Service website has great information on the history of the Post Office Department. USPS.com, then go to Forms and Publications located at the bottom of the page. Located Publication 100, Postal Role in U.S. 1775-2006 consists of eighty-seven pages. Page 72 confirms that in 1855 registered mail and prepayment of postage were instituted.

John A. "Snowshoe" Thompson
Pioneer Mail Carrier of the Sierra

Notes

CHAPTER 1

1 Alverna (Thompson) Robinson and Dorothy Foss, *History Of The Rue Family 1759-1984: A Norwegian Immigrant and its American Born Descendants*, copy.
[2] Dan De Quille, "The Skiing Mailman of the Sierra," *Overland Monthly* (October 1886)
[3] Nina Eggen MacLeod, spelling and translation.
[4] http://homepages.rootsweb.ancestry.com/~norway/
[5] Jon Haukaas, *Snowshoe Thompson*, 170.
[6] Ibid., 187.
[7] Ibid.
[8] Robinson and Foss, 6.
[9] Ibid., 4.
[10] Haukaas, 187.
[11] Robinson and Foss, 63.
[12] Haukaas, 187.
[13] Robinson and Foss, 3.
[14] Ibid., 63.
[15] Ibid., 4, and Haukaas, 187.
[16] Robinson and Foss, 55.
[17] Ibid., 3.
[18] Ibid.
[19] Ibid.
[20] Ibid.
[21] Ibid., 5.
[22] Ibid.
[23] Ibid.

NOTES

[24] Ibid.
[25] Ibid.
[26] MacLeod, spelling.
[27] Andress Svalestuen, vol. 29, 52.
[28] Ibid., footnote, 40.
[29] Robinson and Foss, 5.

CHAPTER 2

[1] Haukaas, 194.
[2] Dr. Kenneth O. Bjork, *West of the Great Divide: Norwegian Migration to the Pacific Coast, 1847-1893.*
[3] Gene Estensen, "Snowshoe Thompson to Find a Better Destiny," *Telesoga*, (June 2, 2001), unnumbered page 6.
[4] Robinson and Foss, 667.
[5] Evelyn Dangberg Teal, *Flying Snowshoes*, 8.
[6] Haukaas, 195.
[7] Ibid.

CHAPTER 3

[1] J. S. Holliday, *The World Rushed In; The California Gold Rush Experience*, 297.
[2] Howard R. Lamar, "Louisiana Purchase," 682.
[3] Melvin Clay Jacobs, *Winning Oregon*, 195.
[4] New Mexico Statutes, 1963, annotated, vol. 1, sec. 5, art. II.
[5] Estensen, unnumbered page 5.
[6] Haukaas, 195.
[7] Merrill J. Mattes, *Platte River Road Narratives*, 3.
[8] Ibid., 3.
[9] Frank Tortorich, Jr., *Gold Rush Trail: A Guide to the Carson River Route of the Emigrant Trail*, 1-8. See Appendix A.
[10] George R. Stewart, *The California Trail, An Epic with

John A. "Snowshoe" Thompson
Pioneer Mail Carrier of the Sierra

Many Heroes, 189.
[11] Dan De Quille, 7.
[12] Herbert Hamlin, ed., *Knott Reminiscence: Early History of Nevada in the 1850s*, 8.
[13] Ibid., 10.
[14] Ibid., 7.
[15] Estensen, unnumbered page 6.
[16] Yolo County Grant Deed Index, 1, 2, 4, 1850-1870, Yolo County Archives, Woodland, California. See Appendix D.
[17] Yolo County census records, 1850, 1852, 1860, Yolo County Archives.
[18] De Quille, 7.
[19] "The Crops on the Putah," *Sacramento Union*, April 23, 1857, California Room, California State Library, Sacramento, California.
[20] Carson Valley Historical Society Publications Committee, (CVHS) *Keepsake No. 2, Snowshoe Thompson, His Life and Adventures*, 5.
[21] James Mason Hutchings, "Crossing the Sierras: Norwegian Snow Skates," *California Magazine* (February 1857), vol. 1, no. VIII, 349-353.
[22] Hutchings, 350.
[23] De Quille, 8.
[24] Reprint of *Snowshoe Thompson, 1856 – 1875*, preface, doc.
[25] "Big Tree Mail Route," *Weekly Calaveras Chronicle*, February 15, 1862.
[26] William B. Berry, *Lost Sierra: Gold, Ghosts and Skis: Legendary Days of Skiing in the California Mining Camps*, 8.
[27] De Quille, 10-11.
[28] Ibid., 9.

NOTES

CHAPTER 4

[1] LeRoy R. Hafen, *The Overland Mail 1849-1869: Promoter of Settlements, Precursor of Railroads*, 20.
[2] Ibid., 21.
[3] Hafen, 28-29.
[4] U.S. Constitution, Article 1, Section 8.
[5] Hafen, 32.
[6] Ibid., 30-31.
[7] Ibid., 31.
[8] Hubert H. Bancroft, *vol. XXIII, History of California, vol. VI, 1848-1859*, 129.
[9] Ibid., 128 – 142.
[10] Richard G. Del Castillo, *The Treaty Of Guadalupe Hidalgo*, 43.
[11] M. Morgan Estergreen, *Kit Carson: A Portrait in Courage*, 152-153.
[12] Ibid., 186.
[13] Hafen, 55.
[14] Bancroft, *vol. XXIV, History of California, vol. VII, 1860-1890*, footnote 10, 453.
[15] Mattes, 187.
[16] Alonzo Delano, *Across the Plains and Among the Diggings*, 45.
[17] Hafen, 56.
[18] Hafen, 57.
[19] Bancroft, *vol. XXV, History of Nevada, Colorado, and Wyoming, 1540-1888*, 66.
[20] Hafen, 63.
[21] Ibid., 64.
[22] *Nevada Heritage*, Chronological date 1855, doc.
[23] First Records of Carson Valley, Utah Territory 1851, doc. unnumbered pages, 27-34.
[24] Roy D. Tea, "The 'Jackass Mail' Mystery," *Overland Journal* (Spring 2002), vol. 20, no. 6, 42-63.
[25] Ibid., 44.

[26] Hafen, 64.
[27] *The Case of George Chorpenning vs. United States: A brief History of the Facts, by the Claimant*, May 1, 1874, 13.
[28] Hafen, 65.
[29] Hafen, footnote 132, 66.
[30] *The Case of George Chorpenning vs. United States: A brief History of the Facts, by the Claimant*, May 1, 1874, 11.
[31] Ibid., 14.
[32] Ibid., 34.
[33] Hafen, 157.

CHAPTER 5

1 CVHS*, 7-8.
[2] Carroll D. Hall, preface to De Quille, *Snow-Shoe Thompson*, XII.
[3] Bancroft, *History of Nevada*, 78.
[4] Frank Tortorich and James Carman, "The Big Tree Carson Valley Wagon Road," *Overland Journal*, Vol 22, 3 (Fall 2004),90-107.
[5] P. Francis Farquhar, *History of The Sierra Nevada*, 100.
[6] Stewart, 305.
[7] Nevada Historic Marker # 117. See Appendix G.
[8] Stewart, 305.
[9] De Quille, 25-30.
[10] See Appendix I.
[11] Knott Reminisces, 9.

CHAPTER 6

1 De Quille, 4.
[2] Christiania.www.britannica.com
[3] CVHS*, 10.
[4] De Quille, 19.
[5] Tortorich and Carman, 20.
[6] De Quille, 34-35.

NOTES

[7] Ibid., 38.
[8] CVHS*, 19-20.
[9] Bancroft, *History of Utah, vol. XXVI, 1540-1886*, 500.
[10] Archie Binns, *Peter Skeen Ogden Fur Trader*, 229.
[11] Zenas Leonard, *Adventures of a Mountain Man: The narrative of Zenas Leonard*, 110.
[12] Rockwell D. Hunt, *John Bidwell: Prince Of California Pioneers*, 64.
[13] Alexander L. Crosby, *Old Greenwood: Pathfinder Of The West*, 74.
[14] Ferol Egan, *Sand In A Whirlwind: The Paiute Indian War of 1860*, 91.
[15] Ibid., 92.
[16] Joseph Di Certo, *The Saga Of The Pony Express*, 91.
[17] Egan, 93-96.
[18] Di Certo, 190.
[19] Egan, 109.
[20] Ibid., 79.
[21] Ibid., 84.
[22] Ibid., 86.
[23] Ibid., 132.
[24] Ibid., 92.
[25] Ibid., 115.
[26] Ibid., 109.
[27] Ibid., 114.
[28] Ibid., 138.
[29] De Quille, 38.
[30] Hamlin, 12.
[31] Ibid., 13.
[32] De Quille, 40.
[33] Ibid., 41.
[34] Ibid., 41.
[35] De Quille, 43.
[36] De Quille, 42-43.
[37] Ibid., 43.
[38] A. H. Hawley- Lake Tahoe 1883 NVHS Papers 1913-1916 Vol 1

John A. "Snowshoe" Thompson
Pioneer Mail Carrier of the Sierra

CHAPTER 7

1 "A Dispatch to the Sacramento Union, May 31," *San Andreas Independent*, May 31, 1858.
[2] Dowd, Calaveras County Archives, doc.
[3] "Letter From Placerville, December 10, 1858," *Sacramento Union*, December 13, 1858.
[4] "Letter From Placerville, December 18, 1858," *Sacramento Union*, December 20, 1858.
[5] "Carson Valley, New Road, etc.," *Sacramento Union*, January 12, 1859.
[6] CVHS*, 15. www.encyclopedia.com for entire Preemption Act of 1841.
[7] John A. Snowshoe Thompson Collection, Alpine County Museum, doc.
[8] Hamlin, 11.
[9] CVHS*, 20.
[10] John A. Snowshoe Thompson Collection, Alpine County Archives, doc.
[11] Alpine County Assessment Book 1869, Alpine County Archives.
[12] Karen Dustman, *Ghost of The Sierra Sliver Mountain City*, 119.
[13] Alpine County Assessment Book 1871, Alpine County Archives.
[14] Dustman, 119.
[15] CVHS*, 16.
[16] Ibid.
[17] Ibid.
[18] Elma S. Bradshaw, *Our Man Of The Mountains: A biography of John A. "Snowshoe" Thompson & Agnes Singleton*, doc., 7.
[19] Tortorich and Carman, Big Tree Road details.
[20] "New Mail Routes," *San Andreas Independent*, Saturday, May 21, 1859.

NOTES

[21] "Big Tree Mail Route," *Weekly Calaveras Chronicle*, February, 15, 1862.

CHAPTER 8

1. Berry, 11.
[2] Hamlin, 11.
[3] Berry.
[4] Ibid., 7.
[5] Ibid.
[6] Berry, 38.
[7] James J. Sinnott, *History Of Sierra County Volume V, "Over North In Sierra County,"* 254.
[8] "Silver Mountain Correspondence: Silver Mountain, Alpine County, February 1865," *Calaveras Chronicle*, March 4, 1865.
[9] Sinnott, 261. "Mountain Messenger, March 6, 1869."
[10] Ibid.
[11] Sinnott, "Snow-Shoe Challenge," *Alpine Chronicle*, 262.
[12] Sinnott, 251.
[13] Ibid., 152.
[14] Berry, 60.
[15] "Jumping Down A Mountain," *Mountain Democrat*, April 13, 1889, 6.

CHAPTER 9

1 Supreme Court Case Number 5358 regarding petition to the United States Court of Claims George Chorpenning v. United States, printed 1866, 3.
[2] Hafen, 65-66.
[3] Ibid., 67.
[4] CVHS*, 8-9.
[5] De Quille, 51-52.

John A. "Snowshoe" Thompson
Pioneer Mail Carrier of the Sierra

[6] John M. Townley, "Stalking Horse For The Pony Express. The Chorpenning Mail Contract between California and Utah, 1851 – 1860," *Arizona and the West*, Vol 24, 3, (Autumn 1982), 229-252.
[7] CVHS*, 16-17.
[8] US Post Office Department, Postmaster General, March 18, 1867, doc.
[9] 42nd Congress, Second Session, Senate Report 73, to accompany bill S 806, doc.
[10] Case of George Chorpenning v. the United States, 20.
[11] Ibid.
[12] *Sacramento Union*, December 10, 1858, 2, c 1.
[13] Case of George Chorpenning v. the United States, 32.
[14] Raymond W. Settle and Mary Lund, *War Drums and Wagon Wheels, The Story of Russell, Majors, and Waddell*, 42.
[15] Ibid.
[16] Hafen, 147.
[17] Settle, 109.
[18] Ibid., 110.
[19] Ibid., 113.
[20] Di Certo, 193.
[21] Ibid.
[22] Settle, 167.
[23] De Quille, 53-54.
[24] Eva Scarselli, *The Mark of the Snowshoe*, 57.
[25] John A. Snowshoe Thompson Collection, El Dorado County Museum, doc.
[26] Ibid.
[27] Ibid.

CHAPTER 10

1. CVHS*, 20.
[2] Alpine County Board of Supervisors minutes, Book A, Alpine County Archives, 1.

NOTES

³ Ibid., September 9, 1869, minutes, 248.
⁴ Ibid., 305.
⁵ Ibid., 314, 320, 325.
⁶ Ibid., 328.
⁷ Ibid., 327.
⁸ Ibid., 356.
⁹ Ibid., 377.
¹⁰ Ibid., 415.
¹¹ "Recalling the California of Snowshoe Thompson," *Sacramento Bee*, Sunday, February 21, 1993.
¹² Evelyn Dangberg Teal, *Flying Snowshoes*.
¹³ Grace Thompson, letter, copy in El Dorado County Historical Museum.
¹⁴ Bradshaw, 8.
¹⁵ Ibid.
¹⁶ CVHS*, 22.
¹⁷ "Death of Snow-shoe Thompson" *New York Times*, May 27, 1876.
¹⁸ CVHS, 22
¹⁹ 1870 Assessment Book, Alpine County Archives.
²⁰ Ibid.
²¹ Ibid.
²² 1879 Assessment Book, Alpine County Archives.
²³ Ibid.
²⁴ CVHS*, 22.

CHAPTER 11

1 John A. Snowshoe Thompson Collection, Douglas County Historical Society, Carson Valley Museum and Cultural Center, doc.
² Ibid.
³ Judge Frazier, Vice Noble Grand Humbug, Lucinda Jane Chapter, *History And Ritual Of E. Clampus Vitus A Non Clamper Guide To Clamperdom.*
⁴ Judge Frazier.

John A. "Snowshoe" Thompson
Pioneer Mail Carrier of the Sierra

[5] John A. Snowshoe Thompson Collection, El Dorado County Historical Museum.
[6] Ibid.
[7] "Bicentennial Event," *Reno Evening Gazette*, January 1, 1976.
[8] John Watson, "Bicentennial Event, Mail Carry, Re-enactment," *Far West News*, February 15, 1976 issue. Permission to copy given by John Watson.
[9] "Boreal Ridge," *Sierra Sun Bonanza*, May 19, 1976, Truckee, CA. Snowshoe Collection, Western American SkiSport Museum, doc.
[10] John A. Snowshoe Thompson Collection, Alpine County Museum, doc.
[11] Ibid.
[12] W. F. Skyhawk, Hubert Hamlin's pen name, editor of the *Knott Reminisces*. John A. Snowshoe Thompson Collection, Alpine County Museum.
[13] John A. Snowshoe Thompson Collection, Douglas County Historical Society, , doc.
[14] Ibid.
[15] John A. Snowshoe Thompson Collection, Alpine County Museum, Carson Valley Museum and Cultural Center, doc.
[16] Sue Knight, secretary of the Genoa, NV, based Friends of Snowshoe Thompson, provided this information.
[17] Submitted by Sue Knight.
[18] John A. Snowshoe Thompson Collection, Douglas County Historical Society, Carson Valley Museum and Cultural Center, doc.
[19] Ibid., doc.
[20] Hamlin, Snowshoe Thompson Collection, Alpine County Museum.

* Note: (CVHS) Carson Valley Historical Society Publication Committee

John A. "Snowshoe" Thompson
Pioneer Mail Carrier of the Sierra

Bibliography

"1857, A Good Appointment." *San Andreas Independent.* May 1, 1858. Calaveras County Historical Museum, San Andreas, CA.

42nd Congress, Second Session, Senate Report 73 to accompany bill S 806. El Dorado County Archives, Placerville, CA.

Alpine County 1870 Assessment Book. Alpine County Archives, Markleeville, CA.

Alpine County 1879 Assessment Book. Alpine County Archives, Markleeville, CA.

Ancestry.com. http://homepages.rootsweb.ancestry.com/~norway/na20.html.

Bancroft, Hubert H. *The Works of Hubert Howe Bancroft, History of Utah, vol. XXVI, 1540-1886.* San Francisco, CA: The History Company, 1889.

———.*The Works of Hubert Howe Bancroft, vol. XXV, History of Nevada, Colorado, and Wyoming, 1540-1888.* San Francisco, CA: The History Company, 1890.

———.*The Works of Hubert Howe Bancroft, vol. XXIV, History of California, vol. VII, 1860-1890.* San Francisco, CA: The History Company, 1890.

———.*The Works of Hubert Howe Bancroft, vol. XXIII, History of California, vol. VI, 1848-1859.* San Francisco, CA The History Company, 1888.

Barry, William B. N. *Lost Sierra: Gold, Ghosts and Skis: Legendary Days of Skiing in the California Mining Camps.* Soda Springs. CA: W&A Communications, 1992.

BIBLIOGRAPHY

"Bicentennial Event." *Reno Evening Gazette.* January 1, 1976. Western American SkiSport Museum, Boreal Mountain Resort, Soda Springs, CA.

"Big Tree Mail Route." *Weekly Calaveras Chronicle.* February 15, 1862. Mokelumne Hill, Calaveras County, California, Calaveras County Archives, San Andreas, CA.

Binns, Archie. *Peter Skeen Ogden Fur Trader.* Portland, OR: Binford & Mort Publishers, 1967.

Bjork, Dr. Kenneth O. *West of the Great Divide: Norwegian Migration to the Pacific Coast,1847-1893.* Nordifield, MN: Norwegian-American Historical Association, 1958.

"Boreal Ridge," *Sierra Sun Bonanza.* May 19, 1976. Snowshoe Collection, Western American SkiSport Museum.

Bradshaw, Elma S. *Our Man Of The Mountains: A Biography of John A. "Snowshoe" Thompson & Agnes Singleton.* Nevada Historical Society, Reno, NV.

Carson Valley Historical Society. *Keepsake No. 2, Snowshoe Thompson, His Life and Adventures.* Minden: The Carson Valley Historical Society, 1991. Douglas County Historical Society,Carson Valley Museum and Cultural Center, Gardnerville, NV.

"Carson Valley, New Road, Etc." *Sacramento Union.* January 12, 1859. California Room, California State Library, Sacramento, CA.

Case of George Chorpenning v. the United States, The Nevada State Library and Archives, Carson City, NV.

Case of George Chorpenning vs. United States, The: A brief History of the Facts, by the Claimant. May 1,1874. Nevada State Library and Archives, Carson City,NV.

"Crops on the Putah, The." *Sacramento Union.* April 23,1857. California Room, California State Library, Sacramento

Crosby, Alexander L. *Old Greenwood: Pathfinder Of The West.* Georgetown, CA: The Talisman Press, 1967.

De Quille, Dan. "The Skiing Mailman of the Sierra." *Overland Monthly.* October 1886. Nevada State Library and Archives, Carson City, NV.

"Death of Snow-shoe Thompson." *New York Times.* May 27, 1876. Copy sent to author from fellow Snowshoe researchers, Sharlene Nelson, and the late Ted Nelson.

JOHN A. "SNOWSHOE" THOMPSON
PIONEER MAIL CARRIER OF THE SIERRA

"Dispatch to the Sacramento Union, May 31." *San Andreas Independent.* May 31, 1858. Calaveras County Archives, San Andreas, CA.

Del, Castillo, Richard G. *The Treaty of Guadalupe Hidalgo.* Norman, OK: University of Oklahoma Press, 1990.

Delano, Alonzo. *Across the Plains and Among the Diggings.* New York, NY: Wilson-Ericson, Inc., 1936.

Di Certo, Joseph. *The Saga of the Pony Express.* Missoula, MT: Mountain Press Publishing Company, 2002.

Dowd, Augustus T. Calaveras County Archives, San Andreas, CA.

Dustman, Karen. *Ghost Of The Sierra Sliver Mountain City.* Markleeville, CA: Clairitage Press, 2011.

Egan, Ferol. *Sand In A Whirlwind: The Paiute Indian War of 1860.* Reno, NV: University of Nevada Press, 1972.

Estergreen, M. Morgan. *Kit Carson: A Portrait in Courage.* Norman, OK: University of Oklahoma Press, 1962.

Estensen, Gene. "Snowshoe Thompson to Find a Better Destiny." *Telesoga.* June 2, 2001. *Telesoga,* the journal for the Norwegian Heritage organization, Teleaget of America, Hudson, WI.

Farquhar, P. Francis. *History of The Sierra Nevada.* B e r k e l e y, CA: University of California Press Berkeley, 1965.

First Records of Carson Valley, Utah Territory 1851. Nevada State Library and Archives, Carson City, NV.

Frazier, Judge, Vice Noble Grand Humbug, Lucinda Jane Chapter. *History And Ritual Of E. Clampus Vitus A Non Clamper Guide To Clamperdom.* www.phoenixmasonary.org/masonicmuseum/fraternalism/e_clampus_vitus.htm

Hafen, LeRoy R. *The Overland Mail 1849-1869: Promoter of Settlements, Precursor of Railroads."* Cleveland, OH: Arthur H. Clark, 1926. (Lawrence: Quarterman Publication, Inc., 1976.)

Hall, Carroll D. Preface to reprint of the 1886 article Dan De Quille wrote for the *Overland Monthly.* Reprint of *Snowshoe Thompson, 1856 -1875.* Los Angeles, CA: Glen Dawson, 1954. Nevada State Library and Archives, Carson City, NV.

BIBLIOGRAPHY

Hamlin, Herbert, ed. *Knott Reminiscence: Early History of Nevada in the 1850s.* Placerville: Pioneer Press, 1947. Douglas County Historical Society, Carson Valley Museum and Cultural Center, Gardnerville,NV.
Hansteen, Christopher, a Norwegian, born Sept. 26, 1784, Christiania [now Oslo], Norway, died April 15,1873. Christiania. www.britannica.com.
Haukaas, Jon. *Snowshoe Thompson.* Austbygde, Norway: Fjell-ljom ungdomslag, 1993.
Hawley, A. H. *A.H. Hawley-Lake Tahoe-1883. Nevada Historical Society Papers 1913-1916, vol. 1.*Carson City: State Printing Office, 1917, transcribed, Nevada Historical Society, Reno, NV.
Holliday, J. S. *The World Rushed In; The California Gold Rush Experience.* New York, NY: Simon and Schuster, 1981.
Hunt, Rockwell D. *John Bidwell: Prince Of California Pioneers.* Caldwell, ID: The Caxton Printers, Ltd.1942.
Hutchings, James Mason. "Crossing the Sierras: Norwegian Now Skates." *California Magazine.* February1857, vol. 1, no. VIII, 349-353.
Jacobs, Melvin Clay. *Winning Oregon.* Caldwell, ID: The Caxton Printers, Ltd., 1938.
John A. Snowshoe Thompson Collection. Alpine County Archives, Markleeville, CA.
John A. Snowshoe Thompson Collection. Alpine County Museum, Markleeville, CA.
John A. Snowshoe Thompson Collection. Douglas County Historical Society, Carson Valley Museum and Cultural Center, Gardnerville, NV.
John A. Snowshoe Thompson Collection. El Dorado County Historical Museum, Placerville, CA.
John A. Snowshoe Thompson Collection. Western American SkiSport Museum, Boreal Mountain Resort, Soda Springs, CA.
"Jumping Down A Mountain." *Mountain Democrat.* April 13, 1889. El Dorado County Historical Museum, Placerville, CA.
Knight, Sue, Friends of Snowshoe secretary, Genoa, NV.

JOHN A. "SNOWSHOE" THOMPSON
PIONEER MAIL CARRIER OF THE SIERRA

Lamar, Howard R. "Louisiana Purchase." *The Reader's Encyclopedia of the American West.* New York, NY: Thomas Y. Crowell Company, 1977.

Leonard, Zenas. *Adventures of a Mountain Man: The Narrative of Zenas Leonard.* Lincoln, NE University of Nebraska Press, 1978.

"Letter From Carson Valley, December 4, 1858." *Sacramento Union.* December 10, 1858. California Room, California State Library, Sacramento, CA.

"Letter From Placerville, December 10, 1858." *Sacramento Union.* December 13, 1858. California Room, California State Library, Sacramento, CA.

"Letter From Placerville, December 18, 1858." *Sacramento Union.* December 20, 1858. California Room, California State Library, Sacramento, CA.

Mattes, Merrill J. *Platte River Road Narratives.* Urbana, IL: University of Illinois Press, 1988.

"Mountain Messenger, March 6, 1869." *Mountain Messenger.* Downieville, CA. El Dorado County Historical Museum, Placerville, CA.

Nevada Heritage. Chronological date 1855. Nevada State Library and Archives, Carson Valley, NV.

"New Mail Routes." *San Andreas Independent.* May 21, 1859. Calaveras County Archives, San Andreas, CA. New Mexico Statutes, 1963. Reprint. Truchas, NM: The Tate Gallery, 1967, annotated, vol. 1, Sec. 5, art.II.

"Placerville, April 28, 8 p.m." *San Andreas Independent.* May 1, 1858. Calaveras County Archives, San Andreas, CA.

"Recalling the California of Snowshoe Thompson." *Sacramento Bee.* Sunday. February 21, 1993. El Dorado County Historical Museum, Placerville, CA.

Robinson, Alverna, Thompson and Dorothy Foss. *History of The Rue Family 1759-1984: A Norwegian Immigrant and its American Born Descendants.* Decorah: The Anunerson Publishing Company, 1984, Alpine County Museum, Markleeville, CA.

Scarselli, Eva. *The Mark of the Snowshoe.* Russell McDonald Collection, B- 44. Nevada Historical Society, Reno, NV.

Bibliography

Second Assistant Postmaster General to the United States Court of Claims regarding George Chorpenning's claim. Post Office Department, Contract Office, National Archives, Washington, D.C.

Settle, Raymond W., and Mary Lund. *War Drums and Wagon Wheels: The Story of Russell, Majors, and Waddell*. Lincoln, NE: University of Nebraska Press, 1966.

"Silver Mountain Correspondence: Silver Mountain, Alpine County, February 1865." *Calaveras Chronicle*. March 4, 1865. Calaveras County Archives, San Andreas, CA.

Sinnott, James J. *History Of Sierra County Volume V, "Over North In Sierra County."* Fresno, CA: Mid-Cal, 1977.

Stewart, George R. *The California Trail, An Epic with Many Heroes*. Lincoln, NE: University of Nebraska Press,1983 (New York, NY: McGraw-Hill Book Co, Inc., 1962)

Supreme Court Case Number 5358 regarding petition to the United States Court of Claims George Chorpenning v. United States, printed 1866, National Archives, Washington, D.C.

Svalestuen, Andress. Trans. C.A. Clausen. *Norwegian-American Studies*. Northficld, MN: The Norwegian-American Historical Association, 1983, vol. 29.

Tea, Roy D. "The 'Jackass Mail' Mystery." *Overland Journal*. Spring 2002, vol. 20, no. 6. 42-63.

Teal, Evelyn Dangberg. *Flying Snowshoes*. Caldwell, ID: The Caxton Printers, Ltd., 1957.

Thompson, Grace. Letter. Copy. El Dorado County Historical Museum,Placerville, CA.

"Thompson, J.A. Appointed Indian Agent." *San Andreas Independent*. July 7, 1860. Calaveras County Archives, San Andreas, CA.

Tortorich, Frank Jr., *Gold Rush Trail: A Guide to the Carson River Route of the Emigrant Trail*. Pine Grove, CA: Wagon Wheel Tours, 1987.

Tortorich, Frank Jr. and James Carman, "The Big Tree Carson Valley Wagon Road," *Overland Journal*, vol 22, 3, Fall 2004. 90-107.

John A. "Snowshoe" Thompson
Pioneer Mail Carrier of the Sierra

Townley, John M., "Stalking Horse For The Pony Express. The Chorpenning Mail Contract between California and Utah, 1851 – 1860." *Arizona and the West.* vol 24, 3, Autumn 1982.

United States Constitution. Article 1, Section 8.

United States Ski Hall of Fame and Museum.
www.skihall. com lists all people in their Hall of Fame.

Watson, John. "Bicentennial Event: Mail Carry Reenactment." John A. Snowshoe Thompson Collection,

Western American SkiSport Museum, Boreal Mountain Resort, Soda Springs, CA.

Yolo County census records, 1850, 1852, 1860. Yolo County Archives, Woodland, CA.

Yolo County Grant Deed Index, 1, 2, 4, 1850-1870. Yolo County Archives, Woodland, CA.

JOHN A. "SNOWSHOE" THOMPSON
PIONEER MAIL CARRIER OF THE SIERRA

INDEX

A

Adams, Wallace 241
Alpine Chronicle 130, 132, 274
Alpine County Archives xxii, 273, 275, 276
Alpine County Assessor 177
Alpine County Board of Supervisors 177-179, 244, 275
Alpine County Museum xxii, xxiii, xxiv, 107, 109, 138-139, 222, 273, 277
Alta California xxx, 16
Alturas Snowshoes Club 134
American Lutheran Church 240
American Revolution 35, 211
Anon xxi, 3, 13
Arizona 40, 275, 285
Arlen, Welie 212
Army of the West 38
Astoria, Oregon 37
Atraa Lutheran Church 242, 244
Auburn Ski Club 212, 217
Austbygd 3

B

Baker, Myrtle 210
Bannock Indians 92
Barnard, E. L. 42-43
Bartleson 88
Beatie, H. S. 41
Beckwourth Pass/Route 45, 61
Benson, Ezra 39

INDEX

Berry, William H. (Bill) 206, 210, 269, 274
Bicentennial 208, 211-212, 220-221, 223, 277, 280, 285
Bidwell-Bartleson 88
Bidwell, John 88, 121, 272, 282
Big Tree Route/Road 58, 101-103, 119-122, 125, 269, 271, 273, 280, 284
Bishop 50, 54, 241-242
Bjork, Dr. Kenneth O. 12, 268, 280
Bjornerud, Gyri Sigurdasdatter 4
Blue Mounds settlement 13
Bone, June I. 207
Bonney, Benjamin F. 88
Border Ruffian Pass 125
Boreal Ski Resort xv, xxiii, 213
Bowers, Mrs. L. S. (Eilley) 97
Bowersock, Bill 237, 240-241
Bradshaw, Elma 116, 186, 273, 276, 280
Brockliss trading post 57-58
Bryn, Richard H. 232
Buckland Station 90-92
Budy, Don 235, 240

C

Calaveras County xxii, 121, 128, 273, 279-281, 283-284
Camp, Charles L. xxxiv, 259-260
Caroutte, Eudora 197
Carson Canyon 21, 58-59, 103, 210
Carson City xxii, xxviii, 20, 89, 92-94, 97, 146, 186, 203, 211, 232, 256, 280-281
Carson City Rangers 93
Carson, Kit xvii, 37, 260, 270, 281
Carson Pass xv, xvii, xviii, 19, 125, 218-220, 222-225, 255-256, 263
Carson River xxviii, 19, 20, 79, 89-90, 93, 110, 260
Carson River Route xvii, 19, 41, 60, 80, 119-120, 256-257, 260, 263, 268

288

John A. "Snowshoe" Thompson
Pioneer Mail Carrier of the Sierra

Carson Valley xxviii, xxxiv, 20, 23, 41-42, 46, 52-55, 57, 59-61, 63-64, 68, 79, 84, 96, 103-105, 113, 121, 128, 148, 152-153, 156, 167-169, 230, 243, 256-257, 260, 270, 273, 281, 283
Carson Valley Historical Society 49, 77, 110, 147-148, 187, 210, 240-241, 269, 277, 280
Carson Valley Museum and Cultural Center xxiii-xxxiv, 276-277, 280, 282
Carthay Center 197
CA SR 88 xvii-xviii, 19, 59, 80, 120, 210, 218
CA SR 89 53, 59, 80, 120, 210
Certificate of Citizenship xiv, 107
Chagres 37, 261
Cheyenne 163
Chickasha 215
Chinatown 96
cholera 18
Chorpenning, George xiv, xxii, 25, 40-42, 44-45, 47, 50, 52, 138-147, 150, 152, 154-159, 168, 176, 271, 274-275, 280, 284-285
Christina, Niece 180-181
Church of Norway 3
citizenship 106, 225
claim 21, 41, 46, 96, 116, 140, 146, 153, 173, 188, 229, 284
Clover Valley 102
Coggin, James 45
Coloma 15, 19, 37, 199, 261
Colorado 40, 235, 262, 270, 279
Conaway, Mary Ellen 241
Congress/congress 16-17, 24, 36, 38, 40, 46, 55, 140, 143-144, 146-148, 151, 161, 166-168, 171-174, 275, 279
contractors 104, 140-141, 176
Coon Hollow 19, 21, 257
Cooper, Peter 119
Cottage Rock xiv, 78-79

INDEX

Court of Claims 140-141, 274, 284
Crandell, J. B. 151, 153, 168, 170, 173
Creswell, John A. J. 154
Cumming, Alfred 86

D

Daggett 53, 55, 58-59, 64, 71, 125, 255, 262-263
Dane County 13
Dayton 89, 96-97
death 1, 6-7, 12, 45, 50, 53, 63-64, 67, 72, 78, 83, 94, 135, 166, 187-190, 192, 207
Delano, Alonzo 39, 270
De Quille, Dan xxxii-xxxiii, 1-3, 11, 19, 23, 25, 27-28, 31-32, 64, 72-73, 78, 81-82, 94, 144, 148, 150, 162, 220-221, 256, 267, 269, 271-272, 274-275, 280
Deseret 57
Diamond Valley xv, 106, 108, 110-116, 128, 145, 179, 186-187, 189, 199, 200-201, 225, 233, 244
ditches 110
Dix, Loraine 240
Dodge, Frederick 106
Donner 19, 212
Doolittle, John 171
dope 75, 76, 126, 130-131, 227, 248
Douglas County 198, 221, 263
Douglas County Historical Society 2, 114-115, 193, 276-277, 282
Dowd, Augustus T. 101-103, 255, 264, 273, 281
Downieville Messenger 130
Dritt 50

E

Eagle Valley xxviii, 20, 256, 260
Ebbetts Pass 122-123, 125, 265
Echo Summit 53-54, 59, 125, 209

E. Clampus Vitus xv, 199-201, 217-219, 222, 226, 228-229
Einungbrekke, Gro Jonsdatter 4
Einungbrekke, Jon Ingebritson 4
El Dorado County 209-210, 233
El Dorado County Historical Museum xxii, 27, 79, 276, 282-283
election 177-178, 180
emigrants xxxiv, 38, 41, 46, 88, 260
Emigrant Trail xvii, 268, 284
England xxiii, 36, 113
Estensen, Gene 12, 22, 268
Evangelical Lutheran Church in America 241
Expressman/expressman 23, 54, 57, 59, 61, 85, 101-104, 156

F

Farquhar, Francis P. 58
Feather River 45, 125
Feather River Canyon 45
Fitzpatrick, Thomas 37
Ford, President Gerald 215
Forest Service xvii, 250
Fort Churchill 92, 260
Fort Hall 88
Fort Kearney 39
Fort Leavenworth 159
Fort Union 159
Foss, Dorothy xxviii, 267, 283
Fox River 8, 12
Fox River settlement 8, 12
Franklin, Ben 34
Freemasonry 199
Fremont, John C. 37, 87
Frost, Lester 209

INDEX

G

Gallo, Torstein Olsson 3
Gardnerville, Nevada xxiii, xxxiv, 280, 282
Genoa Business Association 234-236
Genoa Cemetery 187, 195, 215, 236, 241, 259
Genoa Courthouse 188
Genoa Courthouse Museum xxiii, 228, 247
Genoa Rangers 93
Gentiles xxxiv, 60, 71
Goetzman, Dick 210
Gold Canyon 96-97
gold fields 14, 19, 37, 100
Gold Rush xvii, 16, 209, 214, 242, 256, 263, 268, 284
Goose Creek 45, 57
Gothenburg 8
Grass Lake 210
Great Basin Indians 87
Greater Genoa Business Association 234-236
Greeley, Horace 159
Green, James 98
Greenwood, Caleb 88
Gregory, C. B. 136, 180
grizzly 81

H

Hale, Steve 197, 240, 250
Hall, Ann 113
Hall, Carroll D. 28, 271
Hamlin, Herbert xxxiii, 20, 21, 257-259, 263, 269
Hangtown 21, 103, 253, 261
Hanna, Mr. 101-102
Hansteen, Christopher 75
Harris, Megaera 172-173, 175
Haukaas, Jon xxxiii, 12-14, 267
Hawley, Asa 98

John A. "Snowshoe" Thompson
Pioneer Mail Carrier of the Sierra

Heritage Association of El Dorado County 233
Hermit Valley 120-122
Heywood, J. L. 39
Hidy, Ross F. 241
Historical Society of Southern California 197
Hockaday, J. M. 155
Holand, Hjalmar Rued 12
Holmenkollen Ski Museum 214
Honey Lake 89, 121
Hope Valley xvi, xxi, 58-60, 68, 70, 79-80, 82, 119-122, 189, 210, 234, 240, 250-251
Humboldt River 88
husmannsplass 8
Hutchings, James 25
Hyde, Orson 52, 57

I

Illinois 8, 11-12, 18, 283
Independence, Missouri 39- 40
Independent Order of Fellows 199
Indians *See* Native Peoples
Ireland 36

J

Jackass Mail xxxi, 44, 270, 284
James Marshall Chapter 201
Johnson Cutoff 58, 256, 263
Johnson, Harold T. "Bizz" 215
Johnson, Jack C. 51
Johnson Pass 53-55, 59
John W. Riggs 224
Jonsdatter, Gro 4
Justice of the Peace 42-43

INDEX

K

Kearney, Nebraska 39
Kearny, General Stephen W. 38
Kelsey's Diggings 19
Kingsbury Grade 114, 263
King William III 34
Kinsey, S. A. 148-149, 152
Knight, Sue xxiv, 236, 240, 248, 277
Knott, Albert 21, 257-258
Knott, Elzy 19, 21, 71, 257-258, 260
Knott, Thomas xxxiii, xxxiv, 19-20, 31, 84, 124, 255-260
Konigsberg 111, 121, 255, 264-265
Kynett, Les 237

L

Lake Bigler 55, 58-59
Lake Valley xxviii, 58-59, 62, 64-65, 69-70, 104-106, 121
Lamar, Angus Kent 215
Lane, "Budd" 209
La Porte, California 32, 76, 124-126, 129-131, 133-134, 227
Laramie 162-163
La Salle County 8
Latter Day Saints xxiii
Lion, Henry 197
Long Boards 125-126, 251
Los Angeles 37, 197, 281
Lost Sierra 124, 269, 279
Love, Mabel C. 226
Luce, Doctor 71
Lutheran 12, 240-244
Lutheran History Center of the West 241
Luther Pass 53, 58-59, 125, 210, 221

John A. "Snowshoe" Thompson
Pioneer Mail Carrier of the Sierra

M

MacLeod, Nina Eggen xiii, xxi, 5, 234, 245-246
Mail contract 40, 45, 47, 50, 147, 158-159, 186, 275, 285
Mailman xviii, xix, xxix, xxxvi, 73, 216-217, 244, 267, 280
mail route 40, 121-122, 173, 209
Majors, Alexander 47, 158
Manifest Destiny 15, 36
Markleeville xxii-xxiii, 123, 221, 224-225, 264, 279, 281-283
Marshall. James xxxiii, 15, 37, 201, 259
Mary's River 87
Masons. *See* Freemasonry
massacre 92
McLaughlin, Pat 96
Merrill, W. P. 136, 177
Mexico/Mexican xxx, 15-17, 36-37, 184
Midwest 16, 31, 87, 180, 257
miners 17, 21, 32, 96
mining 11, 19, 21, 32, 96-97, 111, 113, 116-118, 125, 136, 184, 186, 199, 207, 256-257, 265
Minke, Scott 241
Minnesota 121, 148, 180-181
Missouri xxxvi, 11-12, 39-40, 47, 119, 155, 160, 163, 262
Missouri River xxxvi, 40, 47, 163
Mokelumne 102-103, 199, 280
monuments xix, xxvii, 196, 201, 204, 240, 252
Moore, Harold 41, 216, 217
Mormon xxxiii, 12-13, 18, 52, 71, 258-260
Mormon Station xvi, xxxiii, 20, 41, 44, 46, 53, 55, 57, 59, 214, 235, 237, 239, 246, 257, 259
Mormon Station State Park 235, 237, 239
Mormon Trail 45
Morris, Kathy 210
Morrow, David 241
Mott, S. A. 180
Mountain Democrat 134, 258, 274, 282

INDEX

Mountain Messenger 129-130, 274, 283
mules xxxi, 44, 105, 156, 159
Murphys 119-121, 123, 128
Myerson, Melbourne Z. 171-172

N

National Archives and Records 173
National Ski Hall of Fame 205-206
Native Peoples
 Bannock Indians 92
 Great Basin Indians 87
 Paiute Indians xxiv, 85-86, 90, 92-93, 95, 160, 260, 272, 281
 Shoshoni Indians 92
 Walker River Indians 177
Native Sons of the Golden West 197, 233
Neale, Thomas 34
Neitzel, Joseph L. 233
Nevada City 96
Nevada Territory 17, 24, 110
New York 8-9, 15, 37, 108, 119-120, 166, 188, 276, 280-284
New York Times 276, 280
Njord 8
Noble's Pass 121
Norway ix, xiii, xvi, xix, xxi-xxxii, 1-3, 5-9, 12, 25, 28, 75, 82, 84, 108, 135, 190, 206, 210, 214-216, 230, 233, 238, 240, 245-247, 250, 264, 282
Norwegian xviii, xix, xxi, xxviii, xxxii-xxxiii, xxxv-xxxvi, 1, 3-6, 12-14, 20-21, 25, 32, 53, 55, 61, 75, 78, 84, 116, 124, 126, 135, 173, 198, 209, 214, 230, 235, 240, 243, 244, 250, 257, 259, 267-269, 280-284
Notary Public 86, 177
Numaga, Chief 92, 93

O

Odd Fellows 199
Ogden, Peter Skeen 87, 272, 280
Old Muskego Church 242
Olsson, Ole 12
Olympic Games 202, 204, 214
Oregon xxiii, xxxi, 16, 36, 37, 40, 121, 268, 282
Oregon Territory xxxi, 16, 36, 37
O'Reilley, Peter 96
Ormsby, Major William 93, 94, 101
Overland Monthly 28, 73, 267, 281

P

Pacific 16, 37, 47, 103, 135, 152, 163, 181, 182, 188, 241, 261-262, 268, 280
Paiute Indians xxiv, 85-86, 90, 92-94, 260, 272, 281
Paiute War xxiv, 86, 92, 95, 160
Peavine Ridge 59
Phelan, James D. Trust 233
Phillips, California 209
Pierce, George 51
Placer Hotel 58
Placerville xiii, xviii, xxx, xxxiv, 19-22, 24, 28, 31, 33, 49-50, 52, 54, 57-58, 60, 62-63, 66, 69-70, 92, 96, 100-101, 103-104, 119, 124, 133-134, 142-143, 146-148, 151-152, 155-156, 165, 167-169, 176, 207, 209-211, 214, 230, 232, 236, 239, 255-258, 261, 273, 279, 282-284
Placerville Heritage Assn 211
plaques xxvii, 196, 201
Plumas County 228
Polk, President James Knox 16
Pony Express xxxi, 38, 47, 70, 89-91, 119-120, 160-161, 255, 260, 262-263, 272, 275, 281, 285
Pony Express Courier xxxiii, 20, 257, 259, 264

INDEX

Portola 87
postage 35, 38, 144, 149, 168, 170, 265
Postal Route 140
Postal Service xxviii, xxxi, 172, 215, 231-232, 236, 265
Postmaster General 34, 38, 140-141, 148, 150, 154-155, 172, 275, 284
Post Office/Post Office Department xiii, xviii, xxviii, xxx-xxxi, xxxv, 22, 34,-36, 40, 50, 52, 140, 144, 148, 150, 171, 173-175, 232, 255, 265, 275, 284
post roads 35, 151
Putah Creek 22-24, 52, 256
Pyramid Lake 86, 90-94, 260
Pyramid Lake War 86, 92, 260

R

Races 198
rates xxx, 35-36, 38
Reagan, Ronald Governor 216
Reese, John 41-42
Reno 162, 186, 198, 202, 208, 217, 224, 239, 277, 280-283
Reno Chamber of Commerce 198
Reno Evening Gazette 208, 277, 280
Republican State Convention 177
resolution 55, 147-148, 167, 202, 205, 229, 247
Rickey, Abe 188
Riggs, John W. 224
Robie, Wendell 217
Robinson, Alverna (Thompson) xxviii, 267
Rocky Mountains 16, 31
Rogers, Uncle Billy 60
Roysland, Tore 13
Rue farm 1, 3-5, 8
Rue, Jon (Anon) Torsteinsson 3, 13, 246
Russell, William H. 47, 158

John A. "Snowshoe" Thompson
Pioneer Mail Carrier of the Sierra

S

Sacramento xxii, 19, 22, 24, 28-29, 40, 42, 60, 69-70, 96, 98, 123, 140, 150, 160, 177, 183-184, 186, 197, 202-203, 233, 256, 262, 269, 276, 280, 283
Sacramento Union 23-24, 52, 54, 59, 61, 69, 100-102, 156, 269, 273, 275, 280-281, 283
Saints xxiii, 71
Salt Lake xxiii, 12-13, 18, 24, 39-42, 44-45, 52, 54, 57, 86, 92, 121, 140, 150, 152, 155-156, 159, 168
San Andreas Independent xxii, 85, 102, 119-120, 273, 279, 283,
San Francisco 37- 38, 45, 52, 262, 279
San Joaquin 183, 184
San Pedro 45, 141
sawmill/saw mill xxxiii, xxxiv, 15, 20-21, 84, 259
Scandinavian Lutheran 240-241
Schlappi, Jan 211
Scossa, Agnes xv, 194
Scossa, John xv, 194
Selby, Elyzett Knott 21, 257-258
settlers 12, 46, 204, 216, 260
Shearer, V. 103
Shelby County 12
Sheridan 114
Shoshoni Indians 92
Sibley, Major 159
Sierra County 274, 284
Sierra Nevada xviii, xxiv, xxvii, 24, 31, 58, 61, 85-87, 103, 106, 135, 144, 146-147, 153, 168, 171-172, 182, 202-204, 209, 212, 230, 233, 271, 281
Sierra Pacific Synod 241
Sierras xxvii, 60, 73, 75, 116, 123, 135-136, 187-188, 197, 207, 215, 228, 242, 244, 264, 269, 282

INDEX

Sierra Sun Bonanza 212, 277, 280
silver 17, 96, 121, 182, 231, 265
Silver City 93
Silver Mountain City xxiv, 121, 123, 161, 178, 264-265
Silver Mountain Correspondence 126, 274, 284
Silver Mountain Peak 132
Silver Springs 90
Singleton, Agnes xxiii, 113, 193, 273, 280
Singleton, Anne Beech 113
Singleton, Samuel 114
Singleton, Thomas 113
Sisson, James 63-69
Six-Mile Canyon 96
Skein and Environs 8
ski xxi, xxiii, 25, 76, 125, 133-136, 147, 198, 208-210, 213, 246-247, 248-250
Ski Club 198, 212, 217
Skiing Mailman of the Sierra 73, 267, 280
sleigh 29, 105-106, 122
Slippery Ford 53, 55, 58-59
Smith, Mark 104
snowshoes/snow shoes xxxv, 6, 20-22, 29-32, 51, 55, 57, 61-64, 116, 118, 122, 132-136, 143-144, 153, 230, 242, 250
Snowshoe Thompson. *See* Thompson, Snowshoe
Snowshoe Thompson Cave xiv, 79-80, 225
Snowshoe Thompson Cross Country Ski Snowshoe Tour 234, 240, 250
Snowshoe Thompson Lodge No. 78 206
Snowshoe Thomson Chapter 1827 EVC 228
snow skates xxxv, 6, 20, 22, 25, 31-32, 124, 127
Solano County 23
Sons of Norway 206, 210, 215-216, 247
South Lake Tahoe xxi, xxviii, 58, 105, 209, 250
South Pass 39, 121

John A. "Snowshoe" Thompson
Pioneer Mail Carrier of the Sierra

Spanish Trail 45
Springdale Lutheran Church 242, 244
Squaw Valley xvi, 202, 204-205, 247-249
Stanislaus 102
Stave Church xiii, 242
St. Charles 58
Stewart, Thomas 210
Stewart, W. Frank 96
St. Joseph, Missouri 119, 155, 160, 262
Strawberry, (California) 53, 59, 78, 253
Sugar Creek 12
Supervisor 178-179, 209-210
Supreme Court 141, 274, 284
Sutter's Fort 28
Sutter's Mill 37
Swan, William 39
Sweden 8

T

tax 110-113, 178-180, 191-192, 194, 236
Teal, Evelyn Dangberg 13, 185, 268, 276
Ted Tiffany 240
telegraph xxxi, 89, 91, 119-120, 160-161
Telemark, Norway 1, 3, 214, 244
Territorial Enterprise xxxii, 1, 11, 220-221, 226, 231
Thatcher 24, 49-51, 142, 148
Thompson, Arthur xiv, 13, 114-119, 161, 166, 186-187, 190-192, 195
Thompson, Grace 185, 276
Thompson, J. A. 61, 85, 110-112, 132, 143, 147-149, 152-153, 165, 167-170, 178, 185
Thompson, John x, xix, xxxiv, 4, 13, 15, 27, 49, 100, 113, 124, 178, 242, 257. *See also* Thompson, J. A.
Thompson, John "Albret" 13, 206, 214

Thompson, Snowshoe x, xiii-xvi, xviii, xxi, xxiii-xxiv,
    xxxii, xxxv, 19, 21, 27, 29-30, 34, 44, 49, 70, 72,
    79-81, 86, 93, 98, 124, 126, 129, 132, 134,-137, 140,
    144, 148, 154, 174, 185, 187-188, 196-199, 202, 204-
    206, 208, 213, 217-219, 224-225, 227-229, 231-241,
    244, 246,-252, 256, 264, 267-269, 273, 275-277, 281-
    283, 285. *See also* Thompson, John
Thomson xiv, 66, 71, 104, 189-191, 217-218, 220-221,
    223, 228, 253, 259. *Misspelling of Thompson*
Thomson, Arthure 191
Tiffany, Ted 240
Tinn 1-3, 8, 12, 246
Tore Roysland 17, 18
Torsteinsson Birgit 4, 9
Torsteinsson, John Anon xxi, xxviii, 3, 9, 11, 13, 214,
    242, 246
Townley, John M. 146, 275
Treaty of Guadalupe Hidalgo 15-16, 37, 281
Turner, Rufus 162

U

Uncle Sam 24, 76, 142, 176
United States xix, xxxvi, 16, 22, 34-36, 40, 47, 106, 108,
    134, 140-141, 143, 145, 147-148, 153, 167, 170, 205,
    207-208, 212, 214, 231, 238, 271, 274-275, 280, 284-
    285
United States Postal Service. *See* Postal Service
U. S. 53, 57-59, 90, 92, 106, 209, 258
U. S. Postal Service. *See* Postal Service
Utah Territory xxx, 17, 20, 24, 41, 52, 86, 94, 140-141,
    167, 177, 185, 214, 256, 270, 281

V

Vaage, Jakob 214
Vallem, Peter 84

Virginia City Enterprise 137, 188

W

Waddell, William B. 47, 158
Walker, Joseph 87
Walker River 85, 177
Walker River Indians 177
Warner, John W. 210
Washington xxii, 37-38, 45, 141, 146-147, 158, 162-163, 165, 180, 185-186, 284
Watson, John 208, 277
wax *See* dope
Weekly Calaveras Chronicle 122, 269, 274, 280
West Pass 125
Williams, Kent 211
Williams, Paul 241
Williams Station 90-92, 160
Willis 52-54
Wisconsin 12-14, 31, 183, 185, 242, 244
Wolle, Kerstin 240
wolves 82-84
Woodfords Canyon xxviii, 59
Woodson, Samuel 40
Woodward, Absalom 40, 140, 150
Wright, William xxxii, 1, 11

Y

Yolo County xxii, 23, 52, 255, 261, 269, 285
Young, Brigham 39, 41, 57, 86, 258

Z

Zumwalt, Joe 199

www.ingramcontent.com/pod-product-compliance
Lightning Source LLC
Chambersburg PA
CBHW071237160426
43196CB00009B/1091